Advance P

"A joy to read. In eight insightful chapters, Ovell examines what matters most to today's human resources leaders and lays out an astute and actionable vision for the future of HR. Ovell's lived experience infuses this book with wise perspective and deep understanding of the HR executive's many challenges and opportunities. Read *The Big House* to inform and inspire your own journey to DEI excellence."

—Johnny C. Taylor, Jr., SHRM-SCP
President & CEO, Society for Human Resource Management
and bestselling author of *Reset: A Leader's Guide to Work
in an Age of Upheaval*

"In the thirty-plus years that I've known Ovell, I've been privileged to have a front-row seat, watching his vast knowledge and extensive career in human resources, leadership development, and DEI soar. His combined expertise, personal journey, and incredible storytelling ability have made him one of the most sought-after speakers on these topics. I promise you won't be able to put this book down."

—Dr. Sandra Upton
Founder & Chief DEI Strategist, Upton Consulting Group

"I have been blessed with the opportunity to have witnessed Ovell's journey through his K-12 education, undergraduate studies, and higher education institutions. He has undeniable intelligence, knowledge, and understanding of what makes society better for all people. Throughout his life, he has demonstrated the personification of the three Cs: Compassion, Caring, and Concern for others. Ovell's life and accomplishments perfectly exemplify Zig Ziglar's saying, "You can fear everything and run, or you can face everything and rise." He is Risen. I am grateful for being a part of Ovell's life."

—Uncle Eddie West Jr., Ed.D
Superintendent of Schools, Ret., CEO/Founder
West Group Public and Private Sector Consultants

"Anyone who has ever reflected on a life journey will often find themselves amazed by a series of life-shaping events that only make sense once you have passed through them. In *The Big House*, Ovell Barbee is a master storyteller who has combined the critical elements of experience, reflection, and metaphor to guide the reader through the perils and progress of a talented African American man who has seen more than his share and has accomplished more than what is known.

Mr. Barbee's humble but powerful insights allow the reader to broaden their own lens, to both see and experience the totality of one man's journey across a number of organizations as he wrestles with the challenges within his own profession and the external factors that add more than they take away. In sharing his *Big House* journey, Ovell Barbee provides a template for overcoming obstacles, silencing the noise, and achieving the successes that come with the persistence of belief in oneself and the willingness to see it through. This is a must-read for anyone trying to make sense of their professional journey!"

—Lee E. Meadows, PhD
President of the National Association of African
Americans in HR, State of Michigan Chapter

"I can't wait for you to receive Ovell's wisdom and insights on life, people, and diversity, equity, inclusion, and belonging (DEI&B) with the humor he is known for sharing with those he trusts. While these labels and terms may be familiar, Ovell has the gift of bringing them to life while tearing down their intimidating walls. He makes the unspeakable safe in his reassuring voice, filled with authenticity and lived experience. He brings the DEI&B journey to life with passion, wisdom, and an open heart to help us see. He teaches us about our inherent blind spots in a manner that one walks away pleased their eyes have opened rather than with feelings of judgment for our inevitable failures.

Ovell consistently reminds us that regardless of race, religion, ethnicity, age, sexual orientation, geographic culture, or other, we are all "other" to someone or a group of someones. And then he teaches us to #UseOurVoices when advocating for inclusion. Ovell's wisdom comes from lived experience at the intersection of the human resources profession, which makes it unique, powerful, and a true gift. He offers lessons in full transparency in a manner that only Ovell can. Once you take it in, you too will feel like one of Ovell's trusted inner circle—and that's a great place to be! I look forward to your joining me."

—Gwen Sandefur
Chief at Loud Minds

THE BIG HOUSE

THE
B**I**G
HOUSE

A Human-Centered & Progressive Approach
to DEI and Positive Workforce Engagement

OVELL R. BARBEE JR.

publish
y**@**ur gift

THE BIG HOUSE
Copyright © 2023 Ovell R. Barbee Jr.
All rights reserved.

Published by Publish Your Gift®
An imprint of Purposely Created Publishing Group, LLC

Printed in the United States of America

ISBN: 978-1-64484-624-7 (paperback)
ISBN: 978-1-64484-637-7 (hard cover)
ISBN: 978-1-64484-625-4 (ebook)

Special discounts are available on bulk quantity purchases by book clubs, associations and special interest groups. For details email: sales@publishyourgift.com or call (888) 949-6228.
For information log on to www.PublishYourGift.com

DEDICATION

"What about your mother?" This was the first question people asked me after learning that I would be accepting a position out of state. This happened not once but on two occasions, both involving accepting jobs out of state. My mother, of course, deserves a whole chapter in my book for her unwavering investment in me. She worked tirelessly in the Grand Rapids Public Schools, supporting children with special needs for thirty years before retiring.

Despite working full-time and raising four children alone as a divorced mother, she was actively engaged throughout my education at all levels and was known by all my K-12 teachers. I remember having a meltdown when I reversed the math symbols for greater than and less than and got a rare zero on a homework assignment. She helped me master the details, and I returned to school the next day with renewed confidence.

She demanded that each of my siblings and I excel and reach our potential in school. All four of my maternal siblings earned at least a bachelor's degree, and two earned a master's degree. That's no small feat for growing up having to take public transportation and having financial challenges. These early experiences helped shape my work ethic and also allowed me to see firsthand the benefits that obtaining an education could lead to in life.

So yes, her neighbors and my co-workers regularly tell me that I am a "good son," and it is my most significant honor to be just that. Thank you, Elaine (Eland Barbee)!

This is for you.

"Let us not become weary in doing good, for at the proper time we will reap a harvest if we do not give up"

(Galatians 6:9 NIV)

TABLE OF CONTENTS

ACKNOWLEDGMENTS

I want to thank God for putting me on this life journey, being ever so mindful that he has equipped me with perseverance, the gift of reflection, and the humbleness to not focus on titles. I am a person moved by impact.

For both sets of my deceased grandparents, the Barbees and the Wests, who had the fortitude and strength to migrate from Mississippi to Michigan, aka the *Great Migration North*, thank you for laying a foundation of hard work and an appreciation for education that will live on in the generations to come. Everything from "how you carry yourself" to Psalms 23, the words of wisdom, cutting the grass, gardening, fishing, laughter, and recipes! I am carrying the torch, and your investment is getting returns.

I want to personally thank the contributing writers, Trelani Michelle and Perry L. Williams, who helped make this dream a reality. Ms. Trelani Michelle, author extraordinaire! Thank you for sharing your subject matter expertise and your willingness to say, "Yeah, but." You have such a gift. I am forever grateful for the partnership.

Mr. Perry L. Williams is my fraternity and "little" brother. We have grown and shared for decades now, having been trained by the same English teacher, Ms. Enid Zimmerman, at the University of Michigan. I appreciate the strength you show as well as your bravery in disagreeing with me 😄. You deserve a medal. Thank you for your assistance, contributions, lifelong support, and friendship.

My village is so strong that I am not going to list names. I have so many friends and family members who have contributed to my success. I love my village. You all make me smile. I will say, however, that my favorite title is Uncle. 😄 Shout out to my nieces and nephews!

—Ovell

LESSONS FROM THE PARK!

Buckle up, because we're about to tackle some tough topics that are often difficult to discuss, particularly in a professional setting. First, let's talk about how we got here and why it is essential for anyone who works with other people to read this book—for example, how the room can go completely silent when it's necessary to talk about racism and why corporate America continues to closely resemble slavery. Although there are several aspects of diversity, equity, and inclusion (DEI), I'm going to focus on the racial aspect of diversity and how many companies fail when it comes to creating and cultivating an environment that embraces diversity and all of its benefits.

About six months before I started writing this book, I was having a conversation with a close friend about some of the things that we, as Black professionals, have had to deal with throughout our careers. There were two things that jumped out to me. First, we are often so afraid of the consequences of using our voices to be heard and to speak out against many of the injustices perpetrated against us that we sit back and remain silent. This silence serves as a form of approval that the behavior to which we're being subjected is acceptable.

The other thing that became apparent was that many people in these positions of power at companies are simply naive to their actions, but this should not give them a "pass"—not from an intellectual standpoint, as many of them have brilliant minds. What I mean when I say naive is that they just don't know that the behavior they're exhibiting is wrong because it was never brought to their attention in a clear and understandable way. My goal is to offer perspective on workplace injustices and inequities so that people can begin to understand which behaviors are detrimental to a company's progress, and then they can be self-monitoring. This can take time, but it is critical that we all get to that point to maximize our potential as managers and leaders in the corporate world. But before we get into all of that, let me tell you a little bit about myself.

Early in my career, I believed my performance and polished appearance would protect me from disrespect and discrimination. Between my education, experience, and stellar evaluations and reviews, I figured that there was no way I could lose. I expected my value to speak for itself, but I was wrong. My colleagues would step on my toes, and I would have to take a deep breath and then slowly and silently exhale my frustrations. Unfortunately,

I was unable to leave that stress at work, and it buried itself in my body, disturbed my inner peace, and threatened to snatch every bit of joy I had for my job. I realized that my mistreatment wasn't solely because I was different.

As a Black man, my path was not the same as many of my peers. I had to learn the rules and decide how I would engage while constantly being reminded that I was different. Now, when I say "different," I do not mean that I felt "less than" or not on par with my peers. When I say "different," I mean that my experiences, past and current, were indeed different—from my upbringing to my schooling to my obstacles in the workplace.

Raised in the inner city of Grand Rapids, Michigan, by a divorced mother of four children, defending myself wasn't an option. If someone bothered or bullied us, my mother required us to stand up for ourselves. Many of the children in my early childhood neighborhood were told to "dust yourself off" and get back out there for a second round. Often, we were told to "handle it" if we had been talked about, or more extremely, beaten up. That was the motto in my neighborhood and household: handle it. It was a survival mechanism. If you allowed someone to step on your toes, they'd eventually be walking all over you. That is something I learned when I was young, and it sticks with me to this day. Regardless of where the disrespect happened, I was taught to handle it right then and there.

Fortunately, I was raised across the street from a city park. At the park, I learned how to swim, ice skate, and play kickball, basketball, and softball. I also learned to play tennis, sled, and, most importantly, defend myself. The park helped me to build survival skills. A neighborhood like this in the seventies also helped you master "playing the dozens," which builds a certain amount of resilience not typically found in corporate America. The dozens is a game of verbal combat, mainly through telling jokes about the other person, played casually and observed by others (which only adds to the stress). It is designed to teach participants to maintain control and keep cool under adverse circumstances and to develop quick and concise responses.

At the age of twelve, I started my first job delivering newspapers. This was not an easy task by any stretch of the imagination, given the harshness of Michigan winters. I also worked other jobs throughout high school, including as a page at the local library, a cashier at a fast-food restaurant, and a proof operator at a bank. I wanted to be independent and contribute to my household. I saw how hard my mother was working and wanted to help relieve some of her financial burdens. It wasn't much, but a little goes a long way when money is not an abundant resource.

When I got to high school, I lettered all four years in track and field, initially as a sprinter and ultimately as a hurdler. I completed three years of Latin and served as senior class president. During my senior year, I was voted best personality and friendliest. My leadership skills and personality would help me as I started to build my career in human resources.

I was accepted to the University of Michigan's Ann Arbor campus, where I first intended to become a news reporter. I majored in communications and minored in psychology. On campus, I served as the president of my dormitory's minority council, served as a resident advisor, and held several leadership positions with my historically Black fraternity, Alpha Phi Alpha. It was a trying time on campus with several protests known as the Black Action Movements, in which students protested about the unfavorable treatment of Black students.

In fact, the floor that I had been assigned to as a resident advisor had been the site of a significant racial event involving Black women the year prior. Many of the previous residents said, "We know why you are here," echoing the sentiment that they were not involved. I always treated each resident with dignity and respect while enforcing all rules to ensure that the floor was a conducive study environment for all residents.

During most of my time in Ann Arbor, I worked at an auto salvage yard directly across the street from campus. I worked in the office part-time, inputting parts, pricing both new and used parts, and eventually handling various elements of payroll. The store was owned by three Jewish brothers and managed by one of their sons. I mention the fact that they were Jewish because, at the time, there were some serious tensions and misconceptions in Ann Arbor about the relationship between the Jewish and Black communities.

Their family treated me with the utmost respect, almost as if I were family. They would allow me to "borrow" against my next check, which, as a student, I greatly appreciated. They were very loose with my scheduled hours as they knew my priority was completing my education. When the store had larger shipments, I would regularly enlist the assistance of classmates who needed extra cash. Many of my former classmates continue to remind me of the memory of the auto salvage yard.

As my senior year in college approached, I was no longer certain about my interest in becoming a news reporter and made the decision to stay in Ann Arbor and apply to the master of social work program. My closest friends were shocked by my decision to enter the school of social work, stating mostly the perception that there was "not a lot of money to be made" in social work, and many of them felt that, based on my academic ability, I would fare better financially in other fields. As I look back at the comments, I see that my career did excel as I learned to navigate corporate America. However, there were still many changes I would have to make to position myself as a true leader and to get others to view me as executive material. I will elaborate later in the book.

A standardized test and a few interviews later, I was accepted into the program, and while taking courses, I developed an interest in human resources (HR). The program had a concentration called Social Work in the Workplace, which had a required course titled Personnel Management. While taking this course, the lightbulb finally went off for me about my desired career path. I knew I would pursue a career in human resources.

I accepted my first position as a sales associate with Steelcase, a dominant name in the office furniture manufacturing industry. Steelcase was aware of my interest in human resources and made a commitment to allow me to move into HR in the future. I started as a management trainee through their PACE (Professional Accelerated Career Entry) program, which gave me invaluable experiences which I still use today. I learned how to present using all methods of presentations, and received weekly feedback from senior leadership about how I fared. I spent the next nine months at their corporate headquarters, learning about the products and meeting with almost every functional area within the business. I also spent just as much time on my personal and professional development.

One of my earlier memories of my career development came when I was asked to give a presentation to the management team. It's laughable now, but at the time, I remember experiencing a form of stage fright when asked to describe the features of a metal desk. I had very little to say other than, "It's a desk." I was clearly challenged, but the feedback I received was balanced and helpful. What I learned was how to prepare for high-level presentations, which entailed trying to anticipate every possible question that could be asked. I also learned that I should always have a firm understanding of the subject matter I am presenting.

As part of my training, I also learned business etiquette, dining techniques, and how to navigate corporate functions. The company's core customer base at the time was Fortune 500 companies. Steelcase wanted to ensure you were ready and represented the company in the most positive light. I had now come to appreciate how important "executive presence" would be for my career development. Executive presence is the term recruiters use in conveying feedback about a candidate—as in how they present, how they look, their professionalism, and their communication style. None of these factors should be ignored when preparing for upward mobility in the corporate world.

As I moved along in my career, I was very aware of my executive presence, which is why I have always maintained a clean-cut look and used the communication tools that I have learned throughout my career to make sure that I exhibited strong executive presence. I've never been complacent, and my professional focus has always been on climbing the corporate ladder and expanding my professional reach. As time passed and the world became more progressive and relaxed, I saw many of my cohorts wearing beards and long hair, which is perfectly okay in today's environment, but I can't seem to shake my old habits of being clean-cut. Maybe one day I'll step out of my comfort zone and grow a beard and let my hair get longer, but for now . . . this is what you get.

My "corporate look" always seemed to land in the company brochure or on the website in some form or fashion. They used my image to tell the world, "See, we're a diverse company. Come work for us." Sometimes it worked. Publicly, my face affirms that the company values diversity. The subtext, however, is that someone who looks like me won't "rock the boat." Ironically, a company I once worked for decided that they would continue to utilize my photograph, and it remained on their conference room wall long after my departure. I strongly felt that this was a strategic effort on their part to maintain a certain image that projected the appearance of a diverse environment. Clearly, they were not trying to hide their intentions.

As I mentioned earlier, I started my career in sales and eventually landed in human resources. My first job in HR was serving as a recruiter. I eventually moved into compensation and returned to the employment area as the manager. I needed more foundational knowledge in

HR, so I decided to pursue a second master's degree and enrolled at Michigan State University to obtain my master's in human resources and labor relations. I jokingly tell people that I enrolled under a different name to protect my loyalty to the University of Michigan. Go Blue!

As I started to build my leadership brand, I quickly began to understand the importance of being visible regardless of title and staying aware of market changes. I had the experience of running into a chief human resources officer of a Fortune 50 organization. He and other team members were representing his company at a college career fair. I asked him why he was there. He basically said, "Let this be a lesson to you, young man. I started the relationship with this school [a historically Black college and university (HBCU)] many years ago, and it's important for me to be out, interact with students, and understand the competition and how we are viewed." His comments would remain with me for my entire career and ultimately lead to promotional opportunities for me.

One example I can recall occurred while I served as the manager of employment. I made the decision to represent the company at one of the country's larger career fairs. I knew recruitment like the back of my hand and went solo to the event. While there, I noticed that a woman was paying close attention to my interactions with the prospective employees. After gathering her confidence, she subsequently asked me how I was able to maintain my energy and interact with each candidate as if they were my first visitor. I said, "It's important for me to understand the competition and how we are viewed. I also get a lot of enjoyment from interacting with the candidates. Most have great energy because they're excited, and I use that as fuel. It's reciprocal, but it's all a matter of perspective."

She smiled and immediately gave me her business card. She was the vice president of HR. We met for coffee the next day, and soon thereafter, she invited me to meet with her leadership team. A few weeks later, she hired me, and I've never looked back.

I've encountered many roadblocks and dead ends as I struggled to navigate the sometimes unforgiving challenges of corporate America. One of the more considerable challenges I have faced is working with organizations that do not honestly want individuals to bring their "whole selves" to work. When I say, "whole selves," I mean precisely that. Who you are as a whole is important for your growth and personal well-being, but it is also important for your job satisfaction score. People should feel comfortable being themselves while at work. When workers are comfortable, they perform better, which benefits the company in many ways: employee retention is higher, productivity increases, and there is higher employee morale. All of those can have a profound impact on the company's bottom line, which is the overarching goal of any business: profitability.

As a diverse leader, my definition did not always align with acceptable corporate standards, and some companies wouldn't accept me for the total person I am. I had to constantly be aware of making others comfortable, which is now known as "code-switching." When employees can't bring their full selves to work, it negatively affects the employee and the employer, and in the end, we all lose.

Yes, I'm eager to tell my story, but I also want to offer solutions to employees and employers. Employees should be comfortable bringing their "whole selves" to work, and employers should recognize and embrace the benefits of diversity and how a lack of diversity can be a problem that ultimately cripples the organization. I want to teach you how to foster positive change so that everyone can reap the benefits, from employees to customers to financial shareholders.

CHAPTER 1

THE LEASH LADY

As I mentioned in my introduction, every company that I've ever worked for has included me in a brochure, pamphlet, or welcome committee package. Publicly, my face affirms that the company values diversity when, in many cases, the exact opposite was true. Behind the scenes, it's believed that someone who looks like me would not rock the boat. A friend compared me to a field worker who got trained by the butler and then snuck into the home where the plantation owners resided, also referred to as *The Big House*. "As soon as they step on your toes, they realize you're really from the field," she said. "You look like *mister nice guy*, but you're not." To be clear, she's not saying that I'm rude or crass. I just don't tolerate being disrespected, nor do I sit by and silently allow others to be mistreated.

My friend's analogy was based on the operations of slavery. Field workers were enslaved Black people who labored outside, planting, tending, and harvesting whatever crop the plantation grew (e.g., cotton, tobacco, indigo, rice, sugar, etc.). Field hands were usually darker skinned with thick African accents (if they spoke any English at all), and their workload was far more physically demanding than those working in the house. What my friend was ultimately saying is that my physical presence can be deceiving, especially if you're still married to the stereotype that darker-skinned Black men with more than three inches of hair on their heads signal danger and/or incompetence.

In contrast, lighter-skinned Black men with low haircuts are perceived to be safer. Organizations that aren't interested in challenging the status quo do not like people like me because I challenge them to be better. The problem is that they don't recognize the problem, so my suggestions feel offensive to them. I may look like *mister nice guy*, but I'm not. I call it like I see it. It is not my responsibility to make my colleagues comfortable about what's taking place on the job or in society. As a diverse leader and advocate for others, I take it as my personal duty and obligation to advocate on behalf of others, including those who look like me.

The televised murders of Trayvon Martin, Eric Garner, Mike Brown, Tamir Rice, Alton Sterling, Breonna Taylor, George Floyd, and countless others were extremely difficult to witness as a person of color in this country. While processing all of the shock, sadness, and anger of grieving these people's deaths, many Black people felt that, even though discussions about it were taking place online, they couldn't even contribute their thoughts out of fear that their White colleagues might see it, resulting in them being treated differently at work.

Then there are the instances in which these injustices became topics of discussion at work. Writer Jenae Holloway shared in an opinion piece called "White People: Your Comfort is Not Our Problem"[1] that her friend's boss scheduled a mandatory meeting after the murder of George Floyd for the Black employees "to share their feelings and brainstorm solutions for addressing this issue within the company." As challenging as it must have been to narrow down how she felt, finding the proper framework to share those feelings was even more challenging.

Holloway's friend wrote her notes before the meeting to ensure that they wouldn't rock the boat and make her White employer regret having created such a "safe space." According to Holloway, her friend, like so many other diverse individuals, took "great care to soften her language by turning words like *fury* into *frustration* and including a message of hope that betrayed her true sense of despair. She did what many Black employees feel forced to do: make their experience palatable for a fragile White audience." It's the elephant in the room—the notion that security and advancement in corporate America for Black people requires their ability to comfort versus challenge the acceptable standards established by the majority. Hence, where is the "inclusion"? If we cannot truly speak freely about our feelings, then there is no progress being made.

When I use the word notion, I'm not saying that it's not true. It is, for many people, past and present. What I also know to be true, however, is that when Black people continue to go with the status quo and don't challenge our current systems, we are making no progress toward resolving and understanding inequities and microaggressions and how they affect the entire business from the morale to the work product. Early in my career, I did what I felt was necessary to make others feel comfortable. Yet, when confronted with an opportunity to educate, I chose to address the situation directly.

At a holiday party, a co-worker asked me an egregious question regarding a stereotype about Black people. To make matters worse, this wasn't a private conversation. He asked this question in front of several co-workers. I refused to answer the question and just gave him a blank stare. There was an intense moment of silence before he realized the offensiveness of his question and changed the topic to something innocuous. Shortly thereafter, he walked away to "grab another drink."

Rather than address the situation at the moment, as a younger Ovell would have, I decided to take some time to digest what just happened. I later emailed him and told him that the question he asked was ridiculous and offensive. I explained to him that if he was serious about learning more about me or my culture, he should have selected a different forum and approached me privately, as that was embarrassing and uncomfortable for everyone. He responded and apologized, which I did appreciate, but it did make me question what his conversations regarding Black people were like behind closed doors.

The reason I bring up this example is to try to get you to increase your self-awareness and to understand that it's okay to be curious, but there is a time and place for everything. Asking a Black co-worker why Black people drink orange soda and smoke Kool cigarettes is bad enough, but doing it in a public forum is beyond reproach. It's also imperative for those who are offended, whether they are minorities or anyone else, to speak up and address the situation. You may need a "cooling off" period as I did, but you have to use your voice to let the person who made the off-color remark or gesture understand the behavior they exhibited isn't acceptable.

Sometimes, people just don't know that what they're saying or doing is offensive, and if you don't address them, then they will continue the behavior in ignorance. Not everyone who says or does something racist is racist. They could simply be ignorant. Silence does little for these types of situations. It can send the message that you condone what they are saying or doing, and if you never say anything, they may never know. I cringe when I hear people refer to Asians as "Orientals," and I always make it a point to correct them. Oftentimes, they simply didn't know that the term could be offensive. Times change, and English, like many other languages, evolves, and it is often difficult to keep up. And that's okay. To those being educated, don't make the same mistake twice, and to those who are in a position to educate, let your voice be heard. It may make a difference.

To change the course of things, we need everyone to be more aware *of* the problem and more willing to do something *about* the problem. For me, that meant getting back to my roots and getting real with people. I'm not afraid to say that we still have a long way to go in fighting for equity and justice in corporate America.

"The Leash Lady" is a clear example of how far we have to go. I had a White female leader who thought it was completely appropriate to state to me, a Black man, that she planned to "keep me on a very short leash." When she uttered this statement to me, all I could do was stare at her stoically while planning my exit from the organization. It must be noted that she did not say this jokingly. She was serious. I was offended on a couple of fronts. First, my experience and education are proof that I am fully capable of performing my job at a high level, and I know how to make decisions that are mutually beneficial to the organization and the employees.

Second, I took offense to being referred to as someone who needed to be "shackled" like a slave or put on a leash like a domesticated dog. There is not a job or dollar amount that could keep me in an environment with a leader who has such low self-awareness about the severity and implications of her comments—especially while speaking to a Black man. To this day, not one of my experiences (and I have many) compares to this horrendous memory.

As a Black man, I knew that if I had become the aggressor in the interaction, I could have easily found myself on my stomach in handcuffs. No one would have asked me my side of the story. I would have been escorted off of the premises like a common criminal. So, I had to delicately navigate that conversation so as to prevent things from spiraling out of control. As an advocate for others and as a thought leader in HR and DEI, I continue to be inspired by making a difference and changing lives. I cannot risk my own in dealing with society's woes.

Some of the scenarios and situations I've experienced are comparable to nothing short of the dynamics of modern-day slavery, and that is not an exaggeration. I've observed how challenging it is for people who look like me to advance in corporate America. As the world we live in has evolved, unfortunately, some of the attitudes, culture, and politics that exist in the corporate office remain outdated and even antiquated.

Modern-Day Plantation

The concept of slavery and all of its implications, rituals, attitudes, and behaviors is something that still creates a barrier of tension the moment the topic arises. Some are quick to find solace and refuge in the notion that we are no longer in the "cotton-picking" era since chattel slavery has long since been abolished, according to the Thirteenth Amendment.

However, there are still some common threads in modern society that are eerily comparable to the days of slavery when Black people were viewed as inferior and more animal than human. Some can identify many ways in which the modern-day world we live in, particularly the corporate and professional world, very much continues to embody some of the deeply rooted biases that existed during slavery.

Caitlin Rosenthal, assistant professor of history at UC Berkeley, studied the parallelism of plantations to workplaces in her article "From Plantation to Corporation," October 2, 2014. What inspired the research was her work of figuring out what companies needed to do in order to make a certain amount of money within a certain number of years. She began wondering how her work was affecting the actual employees.

As we consider the modern-day workplace, diverse team members overly populate entry-level positions, which typically are much more manual in nature and earn less pay. Many of those working in entry-level roles are subjected to more rigorous work requirements and policies. Earning the *right* or *privilege* to work in the *big house* was really nothing more than continuing to work as a *slave*. True freedom was not achieved because the location of the work changed. Basic human rights were denied for both those working in the field and in the *big house*.

Rosenthal noticed the connection between how big plantations in the South and in the Caribbean managed their accounting were advanced for their time. Often, the owner of the plantation lived hundreds or even thousands of miles away, so they relied on overseers to manage the day-to-day supervising and accounting. This distance helped the plantation owner avoid having to see the ugliness of slavery. They weren't forced to see the enslaved people as humans. After all, they weren't getting pictures; they were getting productivity reports. "[V]ariables such a slave's age, time, and punishment were added into calculations to maximize profit. . . . 'Neat columns of lines and numbers defining productivity were covering up this very violent and inhumane system,' Rosenthal says."[2] Let us remember that behind each employee number is a person and a name. While we focus on productivity and performance, meeting the financial goals requires the collective efforts of human beings.

The point of this research, ultimately, is to prove how a company's management processes can disconnect them from the humanity of the employees. You can't invite someone to bring their full, most authentic selves to work if they're seen as numbers instead of people. Until this universal problem is resolved, employees have to look out for their own best interests. I will highlight the consumerism model we see playing out as employees have many more choices. Employers have to continue investing in leaders with a lens on inclusion and well-being.

For BIPOC (Black, Indigenous, and People of Color), this reality can be exponentially more demoralizing. That's because, on top of being seen as a commodity, the immediate supervisor often doesn't expect you to speak up about injustices around toxic work cultures, inequitable wages, etc. There's an understanding in the Black community that Black people have to work twice as hard and be twice as good just to earn a seat at the table. Statements like these have been instilled in minorities for generations, and for good reason. As I mentioned earlier, entry-level and lower-level positions are still highly saturated with people of color. As you move up the ranks to mid- and executive-level positions, diversity thins out significantly.

Regarding wage gaps, the Pew Research Center released a 2020 study that determined that the pay disparity in this country has remained consistent over the past fifteen-plus years. The continued disparity in wages and earnings highlights that there is still more work that needs to be done. "In 2020, women earned 84% of what men earned . . . of median hourly earnings of both full- and part-time workers. Based on this estimate, it would take an extra forty-two days of work for women to earn what men did in 2020."[3] I am certain that not many would sign up knowingly to work more time for less pay. The pandemic highlighted the disparate impacts that many populations face. The reality of intersectionality makes these disparities even more drastic for women of color. See the chart below from the Center for American Progress.

The gender wage gap is much wider for most women of color

Comparing 2020 median earnings of full-time, year-round workers by race/ethnicity and sex

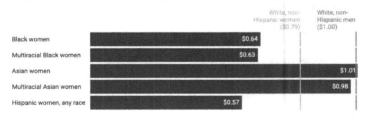

Note: The gender wage gap is calculated by finding the ratio of women's and men's median earnings for full-time, year-round workers and then taking the difference. People who have identified as Hispanic or Latino may be of any race.

Source: For all groups, authors calculated the gender wage gap using data from U.S. Census Bureau, "Current Population Survey: PINC-05. Work Experience-People 15 Years Old and Over, by Total Money Earnings, Age, Race, Hispanic Origin, Sex, and Disability Status: 2020," available at https://www.census.gov/data/tables/time-series/demo/income-poverty/cps-pinc/pinc-05.html (last accessed September 2021).

This data is not intended to overlook the disparities that men face. The inequities aren't as extreme as they are for women, but they are still present. Black men, for instance, "earned 76% of what White men earned in the first quarter of 2022, and Latinos earned 75%. . . . White men fill 35% of entry-level roles and 62% of C-suite roles." While representation for White men increases at each job level, it does the opposite for Black and Latino men, "as they fill 17% of entry-level roles and only 13% of C-suite roles."[4]

As the chart from Equal Rights Advocates below suggests, if you identify as Black or Latinx, you'll feel the pressure significantly more than your White peers. Struggling through debt, discrimination, childcare obstacles, inadequate pay, and healthcare challenges makes keeping your head above water sometimes impossible.

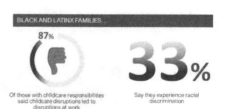

BLACK AND LATINX FAMILIES...

Families Under Pressure and Underwater

The themes from the survey are compelling. The inadequacy of work, the pressures of childcare, the burden of debt, and scant avenues to building assets for families.

87% Of those with childcare responsibilities said childcare disruptions led to disruptions at work

33% Say they experience racial discrimination

55% Have childcare responsibilities

83% Said their current or most recent work experience came with: inadequate pay and benefits, unreliable hours and poor working conditions

92% Delayed a career change/advancement or obtaining healthcare due to changes in economic circumstances

77% Experienced one or more of the following forms of discrimination at work: racial, gender, parenting and immigration status

Maintaining the Status Quo

Social ills like racism and sexism operate on a range of levels, from interpersonal to institutional or structural. Someone on the job calling a Black employee a monkey is an example of interpersonal racism. We can point to one person in this instance who caused the problem, terminate that person, and now the problem is seemingly eradicated when, in fact, if this problem wasn't addressed properly, it was just moved from one company to another. It's essential to not just eliminate the problem from your environment, but it's imperative to educate the offender so that the behavior can be stopped.

Remember what I said. Not all people who say racist things are racists. Maybe they're just ignorant. Structural racism, on the other hand, is much more complex. I've often heard it compared to an iceberg. Name-calling would be the tip of the iceberg, but that which is below the surface of the water is the structural racism. It's harder to eliminate because there isn't one person to blame.

When we're talking about structural racism, we're mainly talking about policies. That's where real change occurs, so naturally, that's also where the most resistance thrives. Examples of structural racism in corporate America include not being hired because your name is too ethnic, limited career advancement despite qualifications, inequitable compensation, poorly resourced diversity and inclusion initiatives, etc. The focus of my recommendations to "do better" tends to fall in this category—fixing the systems that are typically structural.

Many leaders in corporate America are not interested in challenging the status quo but instead prefer to keep things the way they are, because to them, there is no problem. It's the easy thing to do, keeping everything familiar to you. What we don't understand, we often fear. When we fear it, we want to control it or keep it as far away from ourselves as possible. A popular means of controlling that fear in corporate America is tokenism. According to *Oxford Languages*, tokenism is the "practice of making only a perfunctory or symbolic effort to do a particular thing, especially by recruiting a small number of people from underrepresented groups in order to give the appearance of sexual or racial equality within a workforce."

Organizations that employ tokenism aren't interested in actually fixing the problem; they just want to give the appearance of being diverse and inclusive. It's their way of keeping diversity on a short leash. They hire a few "safe looking" Blacks and use them in their marketing materials and on their websites. This gives their customers the impression that the company is progressive and should be looked at in a more favorable light than some of its competitors, who may not have such an outward display of diversity.

Examples of tokenism in the workplace include hiring only a small fraction of minority candidates to make it look like the company is pro-DEI, inviting employees to presentations because of their race or gender, and posting images of employees in marketing materials that don't reflect the actual employee population (i.e., out of the five employees in the picture, one is Black, one is Asian, two are women, and one is a White man, when White men actually comprise 62 percent of employees at the company). Those are just a few examples of how companies use tokenism to their advantage.

When you look "under the hood" of many of these so-called diverse companies, you'll find a much different picture than the one they are displaying. Unfortunately, many candidates don't find out about the company's lack of diversity until they actually join the organization. Asking a prospective employer about its demographic numbers in an interview will likely cause one to receive a letter that reads, "Thank you for your application. Unfortunately, we found a candidate whose experience and background better suit our needs for the position." It's sad, but it's true. Typically, diverse team members overly populate in entry-level hourly positions, and the representation begins to drastically reduce as you look at leadership levels in companies. Data must be presented by all leadership levels to tell the whole story and truly understand the demographic makeup of the specific workforce.

Many organizations' diversity numbers look something like this:

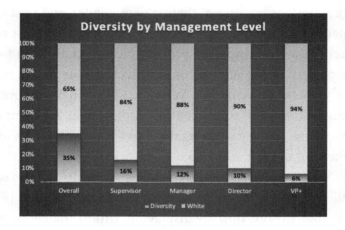

You will notice a steady decline in diversity as the management level increases. There are many reasons behind the statistics found in the chart, but there are three in particular that I want to address. Let's tackle them one at a time.

One could argue that the reason why there is so little diversity at or above the VP level (typically the C-Suite) is that the talent pool of diverse candidates at that level just isn't that large. I've heard that argument made, and it has no sound basis in fact. I always offer a rebuttal by challenging their recruiting process. Organizations need to "peel away" each step of the hiring process (i.e., the system) and examine their policies, procedures, and practices. The systems contribute to disparate outcomes. So, they don't change their processes, and as a result, their organization continues to look homogenous.

Since we're tackling the tough topic of race, let's go there. Rather than recruiting at particular schools where enrollment of people of color tends to be extremely low, companies could target their recruiting efforts at HBCUs (historically Black colleges and universities). Broaden your net and catch a wider range of talent. To use a swimming analogy, it's not about the pool; it's about where you choose to swim. Many companies, obviously, choose to swim in a pool that makes them comfortable but lacks diversity. Achieving diversity isn't easy. It takes effort, and companies that "get it" put in the effort to make sure their organization is reaping the benefits of a diverse workforce at all levels.

The other reason behind the staggering numbers is what is known as unconscious bias. Unconscious bias occurs when there is an act of prejudice or discrimination against a person or group of people that prevents them from having access to the same privileges as a particular group solely based on human nature and our desire to surround ourselves with individuals who share the same race or gender, for example.

As I mentioned a few times now, not all people who do racist things are racist. Unconscious bias can occur with gender as well, but the focus of this book is primarily on race. However, it can apply to almost anything that creates similarities and differences between people. It's natural for us to want to be around like-minded people. People join alumni associations because they all have something in common: allegiance to the university they attended. People join book clubs because they all share the same love for reading books. We all have friends because we share a lot in common. Sure, there will be things on which you will have differing opinions, but there is enough common ground to forge a friendship. When you have a lot in common, you feel comfortable. Let's call this finding a common denominator, referenced later in the book.

Unconscious bias is really about creating an environment in which you are comfortable. By doing so, however, you don't allow for diversity: diversity in socioeconomic backgrounds, diversity in religions, diversity in work experience, and diversity in education. As a result, you create a homogenous group that isn't challenged by other thoughts and opinions, which could lead to better decisions. Better decisions lead to a more solid business model, which leads to higher profits, which lead to higher bonuses, which lead to higher job satisfaction and a lower employee turnover rate. As I have heard many times, you have to learn how to be comfortable with being uncomfortable. We should not avoid conversations just because people will be uncomfortable.

Finally, the third reason the diversity numbers are so low in leadership is performance stereotyping. Performance stereotyping refers to the act of assuming that a particular group of people performs similarly based on one's preconceived notions. In the case of Blacks, we are perceived to be lower-performing individuals. Therefore, hiring a Black supervisor causes some to believe that they're not hiring the most qualified individual because Blacks are seen, by some, as unable to perform technical or high-level jobs at the same intellectual level as their White counterparts.

The basis of performance stereotyping is deep-rooted. Blacks have been at an economic disadvantage for hundreds of years. It is only recently that Blacks have been able to afford some of the luxuries that Whites have enjoyed. This is because more and more Blacks have access to high-quality education, which leads to better jobs and higher incomes for Black families, but there is still a high mountain to climb. Although we're able to get into the building, our advancement opportunities are limited. And, despite having made a lot of progress economically, there is still a large swath of the Black population that lives in areas with schools that are ranked on the lower end of the spectrum for a multitude of reasons, funding being one.

Since many Black children live in these areas with low-rated schools, their access to the quality of education that many White children are afforded is significantly lower. The Black children's exposure to certain ideas and experiences is limited. All of these play a role in their ability to perform well on the standardized tests that are often used as a criterion for financial aid and admittance into college, particularly to some of the larger, more prestigious universities.

According to Brookings.edu, with regard to math scores on the SAT, of those students who scored above 700, 45% were White, 43% were Asian, 6% were Latino, and only 1% were Black.[5] These numbers are staggering, and although Black children performed much worse on the SAT than White and Asian children, this does not mean that they have a lower intellectual capacity. It simply means that the schools that they attended could not afford to equip them properly for the SAT, and that they may have had less access to courses that help teach students how to be successful on these standardized tests. Performance on those tests has very little to do with determining one's ceiling of learning and success. Still, it is a gating element that has continued to deny Blacks opportunities to attend some of the more prestigious universities, and it feeds into the stereotype that Blacks are intellectually inferior to Asians and Whites.

In a way, this is related to unconscious bias because I would hope that these thoughts regarding performance stereotyping aren't outwardly spoken, but subconsciously, this plays a large role in the ability for Blacks to advance beyond the individual contributor level in many of these larger and more successful companies.

If the business isn't changing, then it isn't growing— not financially, as we see many large companies continuing to grow their profits despite having a work environment that lacks diversity, but culturally. Many companies seem to be change-averse, but change is inevitable. Policies and practices that worked with Generation X, baby boomers, or those prior likely won't work the same with millennials and the latter groups. There's a cost to refusing to challenge the way things have been going and reimagining and implementing the necessary steps to take your company to the next level. We'll cover that in Chapters 4 and 5.

CHAPTER 2

THIS LITTLE LIGHT OF MINE

One day, prior to taking on a new position, a pastor and friend took me aside to pray for me. His powerful intercession also came with some prophetic words of encouragement that resonate with me to this very day. He said that the Lord was intentionally keeping my mind crisp and my body youthful to deal with the challenges I face as a diverse leader. I have always taken pride in my physical appearance, but it wasn't until he spoke of it in this context that I realized that God had given me a gift that came with a much higher purpose.

I need to be healthy so I can extend my time on this earth and maximize my ability to travel and speak to people and companies so that we can move forward and progress together with equity. No one is asking for a handout. We just want to be treated fairly. That's all we want: a fair shake at life.

He also told me how rare it was to be held in such high regard and with such a wide realm of influence as a Black executive. I remember him clearly stating, "I can only imagine what you have to go through to fight on behalf of us and how rare you are with your willingness to do so." If I didn't know what he meant then, I certainly have an overwhelming understanding now! Some of the ways I've had to advocate for others (and myself) have been incredibly surreal. One wouldn't believe the challenges and battles faced in a space and time that is supposed to be ahead in terms of equality and fair practices.

As harsh as it may sound, some of the scenarios and situations I've experienced are comparable to nothing short of the dynamics of modern-day slavery, and that is not an exaggeration. I've observed how challenging it is for people who look like me to advance in corporate America. As the world we live in has evolved, unfortunately, some of the attitudes, company cultures, and politics that exist in the office remain outdated and even antiquated.

To dive further into this, let's start with respectability politics, which is rooted in racism and sexism. If organizations are genuinely interested in building inclusive cultures, they have to be willing to understand the impact of these obstacles. As I said before, buckle up and get ready to be uncomfortable.

Eighty-Six Respectability Politics

Professor Evelyn Brooks Higginbotham, who coined the term "politics of respectability," defined it as "a form of symbolic violence that offers implicit rules for marginalized individuals to follow in order to earn respect in mainstream culture." I define it more simply as the unwritten rules of how people are expected to behave in order to succeed and survive, typically rules established by those in power. Intersectionality plays a major role in respectability politics. Coined by law professor Kimberlé Crenshaw, intersectionality points to the ways in which our social identities overlap and prove that not even inequality is equal.

BIPOC and/or people who come from a family that has struggled financially will have a more difficult time trying to succeed in corporate America than their White counterparts. A BIPOC who identifies as a woman will struggle even more. These are the social identities that are referenced in the definition of intersectionality. These are the people who are harmed when they do abide by respectability politics, which suggests that if they don't learn how to seamlessly code-switch and fit in then they won't make the cut. Code-switching is a social survival mechanism that Black people have had to learn in order to climb the corporate ladder. Blacks have to learn to be "bilingual" in the sense of being able to communicate clearly and effectively with people outside of the Black community.

Code-switching, however, goes beyond linguistics. It also pertains to social interactions. It is easy to feel left out when having a conversation with White co-workers about topics in which there is very little interest. So, many Blacks feel the need to "assimilate" so that they can be seen as a member of the group. Social belonging is extremely important in corporate America. It allows one to be invited to specific events or meetings that can heighten one's visibility and enhance one's promotability index. Subconsciously, and sometimes consciously, executives will ask themselves, "Does this person make me feel comfortable?" If the answer is no, then that person's promotability index falls dramatically. So, as Black people who are looking for ways to advance our careers, we have to rely heavily on code-switching in order to even be in the conversation.

However, this goes back to the point I mentioned earlier. We need to create environments that allow people to bring their whole selves to work. When people feel forced to wear masks and hide who they really are, their overall job satisfaction is negatively impacted. This could lead to poor performance, or if performance doesn't drop, these people will eventually seek employment elsewhere with the hopes that the work environment is more open to letting them feel comfortable being who they are and embraces cultural diversity.

Higher turnover means that more institutional knowledge is walking out of the door, and oftentimes, you don't realize what you've lost until it is too late. I have had many people over the years leave companies for the reasons mentioned above. They tell me that the company they left is going to experience some pain points for a while because they were the only ones who could generate a specific report or had taken on the work of more than one individual and received little recognition and no increase in compensation.

I've heard executives say that no one is indispensable. That is definitely true, but for every lost employee, there is a tangible cost. So, companies should focus on retention and create working environments that minimize employee turnover, avoid unnecessary employee replacement costs, and reduce the amount of institutional knowledge that leaves the building.

This is not to say that there's a uniform look or sound among BIPOC people or that some did not grow up speaking what many call "Standard English." Many did. I'm referring to those who feel that they have to alter the way they look and sound in order to be accepted.

I'm a prime example. My visual appearance contributed significantly to my leadership advancement. I was always clean-shaven and maintained a low, neat haircut.

Companies invested in me in terms of business etiquette—how to introduce people at a function, where to wear your name badge, how to dress, etc. I learned the art and science of how to navigate this corporate world as a Black man.

With the exact same resume, however, I likely would not have advanced this far in my career if I had dreadlocks or if I had not been viewed as "articulate" while at work. I saw firsthand how having an accent of any sort impacted evaluators' views of candidates and the impact it could have in the "communications" category. That's the true personification of respectability politics. I personally prefer a low haircut, commonly referred to as the "corporate fade," but had I opted to wear my hair longer, I firmly believe that my ceiling of opportunity would have been significantly lower.

Take Jeffrey Thornton, for instance. In 2020, he sued a company for not hiring him because he refused to cut his locks. According to the lawsuit, a hiring manager told Thornton he would have to conform to appearance policies if he wanted the technical supervisor position for which he was interviewing. That meant he would have to cut his locks because the company would not allow him to tie his hair back. When he refused, he was denied the job.

Five years prior, a Black Baltimore waitress was awarded a quarter million dollars in a civil suit against her employer after being fired for wearing blonde streaks in her hair. While other racial groups were allowed to highlight their hair, the company prohibited Black employees from wearing blonde hair because it didn't look natural. The mere existence of the CROWN Act, which stands for "Create a Respectful and Open World for Natural Hair," suggests how recurring this problem is. The act was created in 2019 to battle discrimination against hair styles and textures.

Fitting In Is a Red Flag

While I was a student at the University of Michigan, my grandmother said to me, "Use all your skills and talents. All of the gifts that God has given you." At the time, I aligned this advice with my budding modeling career. I modeled professionally for fifteen years as I built my corporate career. I've since realized that her words of wisdom could be applied across the board. As a professional, I realized that I had a particular look that many companies wanted. I was tall, clean-shaven, with a conservative look.

From a corporate standpoint, I fit in perfectly, but I was too young in my career to understand that when companies want you to fit in, it should be a red flag. You should speak with as many people as possible to understand their culture and determine if it is a place that encourages and values diversity or suppresses it. That will play a huge role in how you feel when you wake up in the morning to begin your day's work, having an alignment with the organization you work for.

In order to feel truly fulfilled and successful—even mentally healthy—we need to be seen, heard, valued, and accepted for who we are (not who we present ourselves to be). Respectability politics breeds shame, assimilation, resentment, and a hamster wheel of feeling like you're never good enough. Employees who feel this way are not their best selves, and therefore fail to deliver optimum value.

Whenever the conversation or idea of someone not fitting in arises, despite their qualifications for the job, that's a red flag. Rather than striving for uniformity, we should leverage the uniqueness or individuality of those in the workplace. I had a supervisor who felt compelled to "give me some feedback." I had only been on the job for two weeks before she felt it necessary to tell me what I needed to focus on in order to "fit" in the culture. She could barely get the next word out before I told her that the organization interviewed me, got to know me as an individual, and selected me for who I am and not for who they wanted me to be.

People spend more time during waking hours at work with their co-workers than they do with their families. So, it's important to build a team that can work well together and feed off each other when brainstorming solutions, but one has to be very mindful not to use "fit" as an excuse to exclude diversity from their hiring practices. "Fitting in" is an interesting concept in that who defines it? It can be used as a nontransparent means to eliminate people from hiring practices, lacking any regard for diversity-related matters. The definition of fitting in can be expanded by allowing more diverse perspectives.

The task at hand was not to mold me but to leverage the unique individual I was to enhance and add to the culture. It was quite an awkward conversation, but it spoke to her lack of self-awareness in leading a diverse leader and the sensitivities to comments that accompany such a responsibility. Every employee is a unique individual, and if we're not drawing from that, then we're doing a disservice to both the employee and the company (as well as the relationship between the two). There are a lot of hurdles that we still need to overcome. We should be using every opportunity possible to get to know our colleagues, who they are, and their stories, which will help to establish trust. Nudging someone to adapt or change who they are as an individual leads to distrust and contributes to conformity.

Conformity leads to groupthink, which is defined as the practice of thinking or making decisions as a group in such a way that creativity and individuality in thought are suppressed. None of these are suitable for companies looking to grow and remain competitive in the market. This can lead to complacency, which could lead to losing one's position in the market as competitors continue to innovate and expand their product offerings. So, diversity is important and necessary for growth, but management has to make a conscious effort to move the company in the right direction.

When interviewing, candidates can hide some things that may negatively impact their decision to be hired. One thing they can't hide is their Blackness. Skin tone is a physical trait that is obvious to anyone with sight but does not indicate the level of one's ability to perform a particular job for which they are being considered. This statement shouldn't even be necessary as it is a given, a no-brainer. Being "Black," however, is not just about skin color. There is a cultural element to being Black. This culture is embraced behind closed doors and within the Black community, but when it comes to being Black in the office, that's an entirely different conversation.

These similar threads exist in other cultures, ethnicities, sexual orientations, and identities, as well as religious beliefs. The common denominator is this idea that we can't bring our full selves to the workplace. Who we are in the presence of family and friends is represented in our style, dress, attitudes, and lingo. So, what do we do in response? We shrink down, we minimize, we become less vocal, we hide ourselves, we wear a mask, and we become less valuable to the organization because our original thoughts and ideas are being suppressed. Why is this so? Corporate America isn't ready to embrace the full embodiment of diversity.

Early in my career, I was the youngest executive on the team, and this would be my first executive-level position. After an evaluation performed by an external stakeholder and consultant, it was shared with me that my boss, peers, and team leaders described me in three different ways: very formal, never smiling, and seemingly very serious. My team described me as someone they barely knew. My boss described me as someone who executes and delivers. Consequently, each one had a very different perspective of who I really was. So, she wanted to get me to reflect on why I was viewed in so many different ways.

I personally didn't quite understand why until I did some deep soul-searching to figure out what was going on with me internally. Because I was young and the new kid on the block, I felt a need to overcompensate in some areas, which explains why I appeared so serious and formal to my peers. None of the people who really knew me (family and friends) would ever describe me as a person who was that serious, so hearing this feedback was an eye-opener.

Like anyone starting a new position, I tried to be respectful and mindful without overstepping any boundaries, and to an extent, I just wanted to do my job. My focus was so laser-sharp that I didn't really let anyone in. I drew a definitive line between the personal Ovell and the professional Ovell, and with that mindset, I didn't make many allies, and I didn't make any real effort to be friendly. When it came to the team, I felt the need to minimize and shrink down and probably wasn't as vocal as I know I could have been because I was so busy trying to assess my environment and simply do my job. On the other hand, my boss was privy to the driven, ambitious me, and he saw an employee who was willing to go above and beyond to get results and to deliver.

In a professional environment, it is expected that people make some modifications and adjustments because this is required of everyone, not just isolated to a particular group, also known as "group norms." Dress codes, policies, procedures, and codes of conduct apply to all, not some. It might be true that a person feels more comfortable in a ripped pair of jeans, tennis shoes, or open-toed sandals, but does that fall within the policies of the organization? Sometimes yes. Sometimes no. But outside of dress code, some environments are so toxic that a person might feel as though they have no other choice but to try to fit in with the majority by pretending to be something or someone they are not. We pivot around the smoke and mirrors all day long and feel it's necessary to dilute our ethnicity or conceal it altogether when in the company of some of our corporate peers.

"This little light of mine, I'm going to let it shine…" is a line from a gospel tune sung regularly at my childhood church. My belief in God has been instrumental in my leadership journey in corporate America. Messiah Missionary Baptist Church in Grand Rapids, where multiple generations of my family attended, gave me the confidence growing up that, even in the midst of adversity, God will provide strength and comfort. I often reflect on the balancing act of separating church and state, a task I could never do. Although I say what I mean and mean what I say, people describe my approach to HR as taking a "human-centered" approach with compassion and forgiveness always at the forefront. That is me bringing my whole self to work.

My compassion and forgiveness were put to the test one morning while driving to work. As I approached the last half-mile to work, there was a driver behind me who was clearly aggravated that I wasn't driving faster. In fact, he was enraged. The driver was erratically honking his horn and continually giving me the finger. What he failed to realize was that traffic was stop-and-go because we were hosting a special event on campus. I was driving as fast as I could, given the circumstances.

As I turned onto the property, I noticed that he continued to follow me. To my surprise, he also turned into the same parking garage. After he parked his vehicle, I wrote down the make and model of his vehicle and his parking spot. As fate would have it, we arrived at the same door after parking on different levels. As I approached him, he said, "Good morning," and I smiled and greeted him as well. I returned a few minutes later to record his license plate number so that I could ask security to identify the driver.

After receiving the information, I contacted the employee's supervisor and told him that his team member needed to report to HR immediately. After a few moments, he entered my office, confused as to why he was called to meet with HR. I told him I was the driver in the vehicle in front of him, who he had been honking at and giving the finger. Prior to his arrival, I had located an article about road rage, and I explained that he needed to read the article, then report back to me afterward. I also told him that he needs to be mindful of violating people's sense of safety and that infractions of that nature could result in his termination. He was quite remorseful and explained that he was running late.

There were several ways I could have handled this situation, but I chose to handle it with compassion and forgiveness. We have all been in situations where we were running late and frustrated because we were stuck in traffic or behind a slow driver. I could have fired him for his actions, which created a hostile work environment, but my belief system and how I was raised allowed me to show him some compassion and forgive him for his actions. We had a great follow-up meeting, and I think he learned to curb his behavior for the next time he finds himself running late for work. That's just one example of many pertaining to how I bring a human-centered approach to my work because it's part of my core beliefs and who I am, as well as what I know firsthand to be most effective.

"Amen!" and "Say it!" I find myself blurting these words out on occasion, even while sitting in the boardroom. My church upbringing taught me that it was okay to give the speaker feedback to reinforce a point you agreed with. I almost do this unconsciously and have been stared at many times after blurting the phrases out loud when I thought they were my silent thoughts. *Take your time! Alright now! You have really said something! Preach! Say it!* These are examples of my all-time favorites. I am not ashamed of myself or my culture. From my compassionate assertiveness in righting wrongs to my reputation for shouting "Amen" or "Say it" in the middle of the board room, these are key components of who I am. Unapologetically! Say It!

An excellent article in *Harvard Business Review* breaks down the social and psychological repercussions of code-switching, wearing the mask, and otherwise not being yourself when you're around certain people (especially those in a school environment or workplace). In addition to everything I've already said, it also shares that "seeking to avoid stereotypes is hard work, and can deplete cognitive resources and hinder performance. Feigning commonality with co-workers also reduces authentic self-expression and contributes to burnout."[6] If your personal or cultural ways do not harm those around you or hinder the ability to get the job done, yet you still feel like you have to suppress that side of yourself, then you end up hurting yourself and depriving the company of valuable input and progress.

CHAPTER 3

WORST POSSIBLE OUTCOME

In his book *Makes Me Wanna Holler*, author and journalist Nathan McCall describes the impact of pressures on Black people in corporate America and how it can deteriorate your job performance. He mentioned that myths floating around newsrooms in the North and South suggested that Black reporters don't write as well as their White counterparts and aren't aggressive enough to handle complicated stories. McCall explains that Black reporters carry this burden with them day in and day out, "constantly aware that the slightest error . . . will be cited as undeniable proof of what White folks have always suspected."[7]

As I was getting my career started, I believed my performance and polished appearance would protect me from disrespect and discrimination. Between my education, experience, and top-tier evaluations, I figured there was no way that I could lose. My work product spoke for itself. But I was wrong. While I tried to work with integrity and treat everyone equally and with respect, a few of my colleagues weren't of the same mindset. They would "step on my toes," take credit for my work or ideas, and I would have to take a deep breath, then slowly and silently exhale my frustrations in the privacy of my own space. Too easily, we can be labeled either not aggressive enough or far too aggressive. I feared the latter.

More often than I should have, I remained silent. The stress of all that followed me home. It buried itself in my body, disturbed my peace, and threatened to snatch every bit of joy that I had for my job. In fact, it affected my health. A couple of friends of mine were in town visiting for the weekend, and when they left, they called me and told me that they were worried about my health. They said that I looked physically and mentally drained and could tell that work was taking a toll on my body. They were right. I had been sleeping two to three hours per night to meet the demands of my position, and my body was beginning to break down. Their noticing of my fatigue was definitely a wake-up call.

"Wearing the Mask" Takes a Health Toll

Paul Laurence Dunbar, one of the first influential Black poets in this country, wrote a poem in 1895 called "We Wear the Mask."[8]

It reads:

> We wear the mask that grins and lies,
> It hides our cheeks and shades our eyes,—
> This debt we pay to human guile;
> With torn and bleeding hearts we smile,
> And mouth with myriad subtleties.
>
> Why should the world be over-wise,
> In counting all our tears and sighs?
> Nay, let them only see us, while
> We wear the mask.
>
> We smile, but, O great Christ, our cries
> To thee from tortured souls arise.
> We sing, but oh the clay is vile
> Beneath our feet, and long the mile;
> But let the world dream otherwise,
> We wear the mask!

Wearing a mask, in the context that Dunbar used it, refers to hiding your real emotions and reactions. The mask is the persona you adopt to survive and succeed. Respectability politics are masks. It was the soft language the young woman used in writing her notes on George Floyd for her meeting at work. It was me biting my tongue so as not to come off as too aggressive. The mask will have you smiling or chuckling at what's far from funny or saying "that's okay" to what's totally *NOT* okay.

Wearing a mask takes its toll, and it's something Black Americans have to endure on a daily basis. W. E. B. Du Bois, in his 1906 address at Atlanta University, called "The Health and Physique of the Negro American," made the connection between marginalization and health problems. He said, "The Negro death rate and sickness are largely matters of [social and economic] condition and not due to racial traits and tendencies."[9] Physical illnesses and imbalances have emotional ties. When my friends called after their visit with concerns about my health, they picked up on something that I couldn't see because I was in too deep. After they brought their concerns to my attention, I learned that I had bleeding ulcers. Ulcers can occur when people cannot express their feelings and especially their aggressions. Repressing one's emotions can take a mental and physical toll on the body.

Headaches, chest pains, muscle tension, increased heart rate, high blood pressure, weakened immune system, constant exhaustion or insomnia, digestive issues, high blood sugar, high cholesterol, anxiety, and depression are common issues that people suffer as a result of the stress in their jobs. The workload itself is one burden. Almost everyone in the workplace experiences it. The impacts of having to wear "the mask" and not being able to bring your full self to work without fear of career-limiting repercussions are added burdens.

A typical work week of five days contains 120 hours. According to the Centers for Disease Control (CDC), the average adult should sleep at least seven hours a day or thirty-five hours in a work week, which leaves eighty-five waking hours during a typical work week.[10] If you work forty hours a week (which isn't typical for any non-hourly person), that's 47 percent of your waking hours spent at work every week. We spend almost half of our time during the week at our jobs. Simply going to work and doing your job as defined in the job description will make you a good employee.

To be great, however, you have to go above and beyond expectations which will get you the visibility and recognition needed for advancement. Discrimination can stall your progress. The stress from that discrimination takes a toll on your mind and body, affecting your overall performance. Therapists have begun specializing in microaggressions and trauma related to racism, sexism, and homophobia on the job. The problem is literally killing us.

A study conducted by the National Institute for Health (NIH) links unhealthy habits and coping mechanisms to discrimination in the workplace[11]. For instance, racial discrimination can lead to smoking, while sexual harassment and workplace bullying can lead to alcohol use disorder. Excessive smoking or drinking will inevitably lead to health issues, but on the surface, it'll appear that these illnesses are because of the smoking and/or drinking.

With some due diligence, however, more questions will be asked, and the root of the unhealthy habits will be investigated, demonstrating that the real problem is oppression.

Then you have anxiety and depression, which can lead to various disorders and even suicide. This creates a compound effect on employees because their personal relationships are now suffering. Their spouses can't figure out why their mood swings so often and unexpectedly. They're not spending as much (or any) time with friends and family. Their loved ones become intolerant of their unhealthy coping mechanisms. The affected employee becomes withdrawn, obsessive, and/or inconsistent. Interest and empathy wane, and it becomes difficult to be around that person. Without healthy relationships in place, the mental and physical effects are multiplied.

What some people don't know is that wearing "the mask" almost cost me my life. I suffered substantial blood loss due to the ulcers almost twenty years ago. Many medical professionals told me that if it were not for my physical wellness routine (having continued a three to four times-per-week exercise routine just to deal with the work stress), I might not have survived. So, I was very fortunate to have the ability to listen to my friends who were concerned about my health, and I am glad that I had the discipline to be consistent in my behavior change, which is why I'm able to write this book and say that I am in great health.

So What?

Before I became comfortable with bringing my whole self to work, I continued to present as Mr. Nice Guy. To be clear, I'm not saying that I'm rude or crass. I just don't tolerate being disrespected, and I will no longer sit back and silently allow others to be mistreated. So, I wasn't sharing the core of who I was as a person (the side that I now call "more edge," including sharing my unpopular perspectives rather curtly). I wanted people to feel comfortable working with me. It had become a strategy, yet, there I was, on the job, wearing "my mask" for what I believed to be self-preservation. I didn't want to be labeled, stereotyped, or worse, terminated until I was pushed by "Ms. Lorraine," a character name for my least favorite supervisor. At the time, that's how I felt. In hindsight, Ms. Lorraine contributed the most to my personal and professional growth.

Ms. Lorraine was one of my supervisors early in my career. She was an unapologetic Black woman from the south with a huge afro who had been with the company since the seventies. Although most of her contemporaries and superiors were White, she never tried to tone down her Blackness and was a true Southern woman.

Here's an interesting little sidenote. When I was growing up, physical discipline was big in my household and in those of many of my friends and other family members. If you got out of hand or disrespected your parents, a physical reprimand would soon follow. Mothers and fathers would find the closest thing in their reach to discipline you so that you had a firm understanding that the behavior or actions you engaged in came with consequences.

Sometimes, we would have to go outside to the "local" bush and break off a small limb that would be used as a spanking rod. Thinking we were outsmarting our parents, we would break off the smallest and thinnest branch on the tree. We refer to those as "switches." If you ever heard the phrase, "Go outside and get me a switch," you knew you were in trouble. But, we soon realized that those smaller "switches" hurt worse than the larger ones because their sting would last for hours. I know. It sounds barbaric, but those were the times. We all survived, and many of us turned out just fine.

I mention all of that because Ms. Lorraine kept a switch in her file cabinet that she would jokingly pull out to let us all know she meant business. She was a consummate professional, but she knew how to reach each and every one of us. Some Black people acquire positions of power with a "me only" mentality. They don't feel that it's their responsibility to widen the window of opportunity for those coming behind them. This was not the case with Ms. Lorraine.

Over the course of her career, she gave numerous people opportunities that they might not have ever been given simply because of their race or background. I'm talking about people who otherwise would've been overlooked because of their skin tone, their name, or their accent. We weren't just passing go and collecting salaries. Not at all. She would not tolerate that. She challenged us and served the truth straight with no chaser, which is precisely how this conversation started:

"What is the worst thing that can happen to you at work?" she asked me.

"I could be fired," I answered.

"What would you do then?"

"I'd pick myself off the ground, dust myself and my resume off, highlighting my two masters, rely on my spiritual side, which says that everything will be okay, and I would find another job."

"Good," she said.

She said to me, "You say you're from the 'hood,' but I never see that side of you, especially in front of mixed company. You're like Mr. Rogers with this perfect diction. You're going to be eaten alive in corporate America." She was brutally honest and did not mince her words. I have to admit that, at the time, I counted her as one of my least favorite leaders. Black America, however, considered her one of its best. Nearly every Black magazine featured her as one of the top leaders in the country (e.g., *Black Enterprise, Jet, Ebony, Essence*).

"As soon as I start bringing my whole self to work, they're going to throw me out of here," I said.

"For you to be the most effective leader you can be, you have to be okay with the worst possible outcome."

In that moment, Ms. Lorraine gave me permission to be myself versus a watered-down version that I assumed would be more welcomed and accepted. Now, I'm not saying that you should not be professional in the boardroom because there is a time and a place for everything. Her point was that you have to be tough and unabashedly yourself. Sometimes you may have to "break" some English to let people know you're serious. And that's okay. You just have to be mindful of when to "go there" and when to dial it back. But, through her actions and words, she taught me that authenticity paired with excellence in performance and displaying consistency could actually win on the job. I don't believe I would've graduated to this level of leadership without her guidance, and for that, I am forever grateful for her wisdom and understanding.

I remember asking her what she would do if someone called to complain about me. She said, "I would say 'Ovell? Ovell Barbee? He is one of the nicest people I know; you must have done something to really irritate him.'" So, I proceeded down my career path with a greater sense of self and a bolder sense of pride because I knew that someone would eventually test my patience. Fortunately, I became better equipped to handle myself in those situations.

Mirror, Mirror

As I moved into executive-level positions, and now when I see Black employees, the looks on their faces would lead you to believe that it was 1962. "We don't have anyone who looks like us in the leadership team," they say. In my own way, I had become to them who Ms. Lorraine was to me. I want them to release themselves from the chokehold of respectability politics while also teaching employers how they are perpetuating these toxic, outdated expectations and hindering growth by doing so. It is the organization's responsibility to invest in its leaders, and it's in their best interest to appreciate the total person and to be consistent in their words and actions when it comes to company values. Not just at the executive level but throughout the organization, diversity has to be part of the company's core objectives.

What's interesting is that, although I have operated at the executive level for a significant portion of my career, Black people looking in don't seem to realize that I'm treated the same way they are regardless of my "rank." Yes, I have the title, but I still struggle with the same challenges they face with regard to discriminatory treatment. My work is scrutinized more, my suggestions are challenged with more fervor, and my education and experience aren't respected at the same level as my peers. So, unlike them, I'm fighting an uphill battle. Always have and always will.

I am constantly proving myself to my supervisors, peers, and subordinates. It's tiring, but it has made me stronger and better at my job.

I'm extremely calculating about what I say and present because my ideas have to be supported by data and facts. I don't have the privilege of presenting an idea or proposal based on my subjective opinion. I will and have been challenged enough to understand and embrace the importance of data in presenting recommendations, especially in the diversity, equity, and inclusion space. I will elaborate more on this later in the book.

Behaviors that foster inequity can be recognized and stamped out before their embers can turn into a raging fire. So, you as a leader can be self-monitoring and take proactive steps to handle situations differently than you would have prior to reading this book. I honestly don't think there are many people out there with deliberate intentions to discriminate or alienate their co-workers. I really don't. I've had enough interactions with people to know that change is a product of education, and the more educated you are about how people who look like me, or better yet, people who don't look like you, the more you will be better equipped to work with them in a way that will be beneficial to you, your employees, and the organization as a whole.

Village of Mentors

"If you learned to state your concern in a more positive manner, maybe people would listen to you."

That was the response I received when I learned that my anticipated merit increase would not happen due to the company's poor financial performance. I angrily confronted the employee relations manager, whom I did not particularly like, and expressed my frustration. Contributing to my stress were the huge student loan payments I had, along with the pressure of having to obtain a part-time job in order to afford to accelerate the payments. His counsel impacted me at the moment and has followed me throughout my career. You must always be aware of how you communicate your perspective and the importance of "word choice."

As I reflect upon my key mentors, like the person above, many were not people I naturally gravitated toward. Still, every one of them became mentors because they all conveyed consistent themes. Regardless of how I may have felt about their opinions, I respected them because they were honest and constructive with their feedback. They took the time to get to know me as an individual and made themselves available whenever I had questions. My mentors were women and men who came from various racial backgrounds. All, collectively, have made significant contributions as I built my leadership brand and advanced my career.

Being a leader is a difficult job, and not everyone can do it effectively. Leaders can bring the best or worst out of someone. Their ability to lead by example is important, but what they say and how they say it is equally important. Being able to deliver the truth in a way that the recipient can receive it is a skill set. Being able to genuinely apologize is another trait of a great leader. We all make mistakes. It's how we handle ourselves after the mistake has been made that speaks to our true character. Accept responsibility and move forward.

CHAPTER 4

SAY UNCLE

A n effective leader, among so many other things, is one who inspires and is able to build teams and communicate a vision. The leader must also be someone who is self-aware, an astute listener, and fosters diverse perspectives. Many of our organizations are great at inspiring and communicating a vision, but those last three traits are lacking. Being an astute listener and having self-awareness go hand-in-hand. You can't have one without the other—the same for fostering diverse perspectives. Until you realize that you don't know everything (self-awareness) and are able to sit with people who are very different from you and be willing to be the student, then there's no way that you can make space for these people and the value that they bring to the organization.

Over the course of thirty years in corporate America, there's been very little progress in terms of cultural inclusiveness. African Americans are typically terminated at much higher rates. Google it across any industry, and you'll find it to be true. Diversity, equity, and inclusion are popular terms that bear little weight in reality. Companies say that they want people from a wide array of backgrounds. They say that they want us to bring our whole selves to work, but in actuality, that's not what they really want. I don't believe that most companies even know what a diverse workforce truly looks like. That's the goal—putting appropriate systems into place that make our workplaces better for all.

Just as there are consequences for employees who wear "the mask," there are also costs associated with companies not allowing their employees to bring their whole selves to work. This includes not being able to land the top talent, having employees who aren't motivated, and as a result, needing to constantly hire because your retention rate is suffering.

Raise Your Hand

The George Floyd video led to an awakening. During this time period, not only were we trying to grapple with the death of George Floyd, but we were also dealing with a worldwide pandemic that totally disrupted our lives. As a DEI practitioner, the video led to a multitude of people reaching out to me and my team asking how they could assist, many echoing the words, "I had no idea the travesties Black people face." Although I welcomed the assistance (as many DEI teams are strapped with limited resources), there was a part of me that wondered about the "new" interest in helping and whether the video, which was serving as the catalyst for the interest, is indicative of other challenges that face our country and corporate America.

Personally, I feel a duty and obligation to help those in need. I wonder how the "awakening," which was driven by watching a nine-minute video of someone being murdered, was going to affect how we respond to cries for help. I wondered how we respond when we hear desperate pleas such as "Call 911!" or "Somebody help me!" Would we take action when seeing an elderly person in need, or would we choose to ignore their pleas for assistance? It reminds me of the childhood wrestling game called "Say uncle," in which an opponent would hold someone down until the other person had enough and "tapped out" by saying the word "uncle."

We can't afford to ignore social injustices, tragic events, and the other atrocities that are happening in our everyday world. It is time we change the way we respond and when we respond. Unfortunately, like many people, some companies will continue to choose to remain silent or neutral, which can be counterproductive and stall any progress that we may be making.

I encouraged those who reached out to me after the George Floyd video to become active participants in the call for change. Terms such as allies or ambassadors are necessary resources for us to "do better." The work cannot be done by diverse people alone. Everyone has to participate in order for there to be real change. Let us stand together, stop the silence, and "say uncle" on someone else's behalf. It should not take watching such a horrific video before we raise our hand to assist someone in need. As individuals, we can do something to make our communities better.

After the 9/11 terrorist attacks, we found a common denominator as Americans. During the peak of COVID-19, we worked together to get through the pandemic that was responsible for the loss of hundreds of thousands of lives in the US. Our sense of normalcy had been disrupted, and through that experience, we found ourselves in need of mental and physical outlets to reduce the increased stress brought on by the pandemic. That collective need birthed a whole new meaning for well-being.

The senseless murder of George Floyd was not an isolated incident. It's been happening since Black people arrived in this country. While the video footage makes it more visible, newspapers, magazines, radio, and even television have long since been exposing the violence against Black bodies. None of it is new. The same goes for what's happening in the workplace. The data on disparities against BIPOC isn't new. The lawsuits against discrimination aren't new. Affirmative action was a response to a consistently reoccurring injustice—the same for the #MeToo movement.

We need to have the same amount of energy and effort towards raising our hands and saying we've had enough of the structural violence[12] that is affecting BIPOC people in corporate America.

CHAPTER 5

THE TABLES ARE TURNING

We're currently in what's being called an employee's market or the consumerism model referenced earlier, in which employees have more options. The job market tilts in favor of job candidates versus employers, and companies cannot afford to miss the mark here. At the time of writing this, there are over fifteen million jobs open right now. According to Josh Bersin, who provides research and advisory services focused on corporate learning, one in ten employee seats are empty.

"Adding to this frenzy," Bersin points out, "the job creation continues [and] Citibank's economist unit believes that next year, we will have more than 20 million job openings in the US, bringing the percentage of seats unfilled to one in eight." Employees have more say in this market because there are fewer candidates. This is the "consumerism" time for employees. They have more choices and more to say. If they expect to survive, employers need to reevaluate their recruiting and retention tactics. The benefits are not all soft. Some will manifest themselves in the form of higher employee satisfaction and retention, which will have a positive effect on the bottom line. Once executives understand that their profits will be larger and their bonuses will be bigger, things will change. Cash is king, unfortunately.

As times change, the rules of engagement also need to change in the corporate world. Ideas also conform to these changing times concerning professionalism in the workplace. Some of these variables are also reflected in policies and procedures. Even with these changes, some individuals still experience conflict when it comes to maintaining one's true identity in the workplace.

New Generations

There are still some blurred lines that exist, particularly when dealing with generational differences amidst the ever-evolving world in which we live. It's very possible to have as many as five generations working for the same organization at the same time (the Silent Generation, baby boomers, Generation X, millennials, and Generation Z). The incontestable truth, however, is that the older generations are retiring while the younger generations are onboarding. The interactions within the workplace caused by such a broad mix of generations all working together can create some interesting dynamics.

Millennials and Generation Z are often considered to be lazy, entitled, and disrespectful. This is simply because their values are much different from those of the older generations, who typically landed "a good job" and stayed there until retirement. Younger generations are more open to change and less tolerant of organizations that take more than they give. Working long hours isn't exactly on their to-do list. As a result, knowing that they have options, the younger generations will simply quit and move on to a company that they believe is better suited for their lifestyle: a company that embraces work-life balance and diversity. They are also advocates of completing tasks quicker and with as much automation as possible, which is why they fully embrace new systems and new technologies.

Then there's self-expression. From a fashion standpoint, so many elements create a vast generational divide when it comes to defining what is appropriate and what is not. There was a time and place when it was considered extremely risqué for a man to wear an earring in any work setting. Now, it's common to see multiple piercings, brightly colored hair, and even tattoos, depending on the industry. Facial hair has turned into a statement of expression. Some companies still forbid facial hair, which tells me that those companies are resistant to change. Attire has become more casual.

Some industries still require formal business attire, but many companies across the nation have relaxed their dress codes. At one point, relaxed dress codes were seen as a "California thing," but now, companies have realized that, in order to remain competitive, they need to evolve. Some get it, and some don't, but those that don't will miss out on some outstanding talent because people realize that they have options. So, businesses need to quickly figure it out or fall behind.

In today's world, the name of the game is *Inclusion*. That entails meeting individuals where they are, which means creating a sense of trust and investing in leaders who play a key role in fostering and creating environments in which all employees can thrive. This also means focusing on individual needs, addressing team members' well-beings, and investing in leaders to build their "inclusive" competency or skill. The "new" environment must allow managers to lead diverse team members and teach them how to do so in a more effective manner.

The Leash Lady is an example of leadership gone wrong. A White woman telling me, a Black man, that she was going to keep me on a short leash was totally unacceptable. Words may not break bones like sticks and stones, but words can be equally damaging to confidence levels, relationships, and productivity.

Pre- and Post-Pandemic

Remember in March 2020 when the world shut down and most places went into quarantine? We were faced with a pandemic that global leaders had no idea how to handle, so we sent everyone home with their computers, masks, and a bottle of hand sanitizer. By the following month, more than 20 million people were unemployed, and the heroes became the front-line workers (aka the essential workers). Layoffs were only one piece of the puzzle; resignations were another. According to *The Washington Post*, 4.3 million Americans quit their job in December 2021.

The majority of workers who quit a job in 2021 say low pay (63 percent), no opportunities for advancement (63 percent), and feeling disrespected at work (57 percent) were reasons why they quit, according to the February 7-13 survey. At least a third say each of these was a major reason for leaving.

Roughly half say childcare issues were a reason they quit a job (48 percent among those with a child younger than eighteen in the household). A similar number points to a lack of flexibility in choosing when they put in their hours (45 percent) or not having good benefits such as health insurance and paid time off (43 percent). Roughly a quarter say each of these was a major reason.

About four-in-ten adults who quit a job last year (39 percent) say a reason was that they were working too many hours, while three in ten cite working too few hours. About a third (35 percent) cite wanting to relocate to a different area, while relatively few (18 percent) cite their employer requiring a COVID-19 vaccine as a reason.[13]

Again, today's workforce has shifted to a consumerism model in which employees have choices and options. Savvy employers are focusing on creating individualized options that address employees' total well-being and paying close attention to the experiences that employees have. Your best bet? If you're an employer, be the savvy one. If you're an employee, work for the savvy one.

The Four Components of a Future HR Vision

I see the vision for HR in the future focusing on four primary components: the people experience, engagement and inclusion, human-centeredness, and an individual focus. Achieving this vision requires a workforce that is engaged and more inclusive than ever before. The vision for HR is to provide a transformed HR delivery model that will differentiate work culture and support employees. Using experience as a gauge and addressing the needs of the workforce will allow organizations to demonstrate a stronger commitment to "people." All of these together will provide a framework for inclusive organizations that foster trust and goodwill. Let's explore deeper and define the four primary components.

<u>People Experience</u>: Today, we understand that employees want to bring their "whole selves to work." We will focus our HR work on people-centric experiences. Experience should be the gauge for every touch point with the workforce, including candidates.

Using experience as the "litmus" test, organizations should define all users of human resources as customers, building upon the premises of the "consumerism" model introduced earlier, highlighting that people have many more choices than ever before. This starts with candidates and includes all employees within an organization, from individual contributors to leaders. In a challenging hiring market, how an organization engages with a prospective new hire begins with the "experience" the candidate has with the organization. The timeliness of the company's response, ease of applying, interviewing practices, and clarity of next steps are all examples of how the experience affects candidates' decisions to accept a potential offer or remove themselves from the interviewing process.

<u>Engagement & Inclusion</u>: The rallying cries for HR in the past were to attract, retain, and reward. Now, a different approach is needed. This broad approach leverages a diverse group of team members coming together to share ideas and address issues that impact the business and individuals.

The excitement new team members feel when starting a new job can disappear on the day of arrival. When presenting to new team members, I would always remind them to remember the point at which they learned they were being offered a job. The task for organizations is to make sure to teach the organizational "norms" (i.e., where to park, dress code, attendance, etc.), as well as leverage the talents and skills and all the other reasons the new hire was selected into the organization. Organizations must have processes in place to ensure that team members who "use their voices" can be heard. They need to lay a solid foundation for maximizing workforce engagement. Examples include engagement surveys and a commitment to action, open-door policies, and formalized means to submit ideas for problem-solving and innovation.

In many cases, employees can be instrumental in identifying operational efficiency gains and providing insights that can help an organization's bottom line. Empowering them to use their voices only strengthens the organization and can help the company to remain relevant in an increasingly competitive environment.

<u>Human-Centeredness</u>: Meeting the "whole-person" will serve organizations well in the future. We will put more emphasis on the "human" in human resources.

In health care, it is common to discuss the social determinants contributing to the health outcomes of patients.

Examples include transportation, housing, education, nutrition, employment, and social-economic status. Suppose organizations begin to understand similar impacts that these areas have on their employees in general. In that case, they will experience higher talent retention rates, and the employer-employee relationship will be strengthened.

Human-centered means we are looking at policies, practices, and procedures while never losing sight of the fact that we are talking about human beings. Unfortunately, we have not reached a point where we can forgo this reminder. At one organization, we had to make significant changes to our attendance policy because it contributed to significant challenges for our entry-level hourly team members, who were broadly diverse. The population contributed significantly to the organization's mission, and the previous policy did not offer the flexibility needed to respond to everyday challenges (i.e., sick children, deaths, etc.). Our investment in a "systemic" fix by changing the policy vs. a short-term approach contributed to a reduction in turnover.

Individual Focus: We understand that what matters most to one team member may have little significance for another. HR initiatives need to provide both a consistent structure and one that is flexible enough to meet individual needs.

Diversity, equity, and inclusion practices teach us to embrace the uniqueness of individuals. The model of the future serves as a reminder of the importance of this statement. As organizations establish or review policies and practices, it's important to understand that in a "consumerism" model, the basic premise is that people have choices and want options. How you pay tuition "reimbursement" is an example—paying after completion of the course may be a barrier for certain team members. A parental leave policy that does not include both parents or adoption could be a reason for someone to choose not to join an organization. Incorporating diverse perspectives in decision-making and ensuring that options are developed as a result will lead to organizations being in a better place to meet the demands of a changing workforce.

With new technologies and the shifting expectations of the workforce as a result of the values of younger generations, the pandemic, and more, corporations are forced to change how they operate and how they communicate those operations. This creates an unparalleled opportunity for human resource departments to play a fundamental role in shaping how companies compete, recruit, and show up in the global market. By adopting these four components, corporate America sets itself to succeed on an unprecedented level, from the inside out.

What Employees Want

78%
Employees and job seekers say it's
important to them to work at an organization
that prioritizes diversity and inclusion

24%
Employees say that their company is
"not doing enough" to address DEI

80%
American employees want their company
to invest more energy into promoting
diversity and inclusion in the workplace

32%
Employees and job seekers would not
apply to a job at a company where there
is a lack of diversity among its workforce

www.glassdoor.com/employees/blog/diversity/
www.surveymonkey.com/curiosity/cnbc-workforce-survey-april-2021/

#QuietQuitting

Bleeding ulcers and losing 240 hours of earned paid time off are major examples of what can happen in corporate America if you continue to follow the "old rules"—rules that applied when our grandparents were in the workplace. Is it really true that, in order to get the same outcomes as your peers, folks who identify as BIPOC need to put in twice the effort and time? I would argue yes. It's sad but true. Throughout my career, I was constantly aware that my standards would be different. I regularly lament with diverse colleagues about being the first person in the office and the last one to leave. We have to prove that we belong and do whatever we can to break the stereotype that we are less competent than our White, Asian, or Indian counterparts.

#QuietQuitting has become a popular saying. Despite the inferences, it doesn't mean quitting the job without notice. It means going to work and performing your duties as expected and with minimal effort. It's doing exactly what's outlined in the job description, nothing more, nothing less. The reason is simple: people are sick and tired of being sick and tired. Employers are beginning to focus significantly on well-being and work-life balance to avoid the cycle of working hard and putting in twice the effort, only to be overlooked when it comes time for acknowledgment or reward, or even worse, to avoid burnout.

What does this mean for employers as it relates to DEI? Considering the current inequities that exist across the board, BIPOC employees are more prone to quiet quitting. If they're being paid less, valued less, and penalized more harshly, they're far less likely to volunteer to step up to help the company reach its goals when that stepping up requires them to do more than what's required of them. Why go the extra mile for a company that doesn't make you feel prioritized?

It's a stiff nudge to pay attention to and to take heed. Identify which employees are dedicated to going above and beyond and the motivating factors driving them to do so. When individuals and teams are highly engaged, they exhibit more energy and investment in whatever project is in front of them. Identify who's leading the team and notice which employees might have already "quietly quit." Employers must keep in mind that employees who feel wanted, appreciated, and heard are far more motivated and productive. Everyone benefits when this happens. So, ask yourself, "What's preventing us from making changes and moving forward?" It's a difficult question, but one that needs to be asked and answered honestly.

CHAPTER 6

STOP THE SILENCE (EMPLOYEES)

I was asked to give a presentation to a group of mid-to-high-level executives, and I wanted to ensure that I immediately captured their attention. I walked across the stage silently, staring at the hundreds of audience members without saying a word. I had carefully selected my presentation attire so that I would be the "silent" center of attention.

As I walked back and forth, saying nothing, I could see the looks of panic beginning to surface on the faces of many attendees, some of whom were personal friends and colleagues. I could imagine their thoughts ranging from "Is he having a meltdown?" to "Is the PowerPoint not working?" My usual smile was gone, I appeared to be stoic, not saying a word, and I intentionally waited two to three full minutes before shouting, "Stop the Silence!" I wanted to "show" my reply to the question the organizers of the event wanted me to answer, which was, "What's the greatest challenge I face as a leader in the diversity space?"

The answer was simple: silence.

Silence is the most significant challenge I face in the DEI space.

Repeatedly, I found that when necessary conversations needed to be held about racism, discrimination, or diversity, oftentimes, the room (mostly filled with upper-management leaders) would go completely silent. Crickets. It was so awkward to experience, and I always felt like someone needed to say something, and I typically had to break the ice. My passion for diversity led to me being selected to serve as a chief diversity officer, although most of my career had been spent in human resources. This happens to diverse talent who are often nominated or appointed by their organizations to lead councils, forums, conferences, etc. . . . oftentimes, these additional responsibilities do not come with further compensation and typically no additional support. Organizations can translate passion into contribution, but practitioners of DEI deserve credit and recognition for building expertise in a field faced with so many challenges.

One of the reasons why management avoids the necessary conversations that push for change is the fear of making people feel uncomfortable. In order to have change, we have to learn to be comfortable with being uncomfortable. I am uncomfortable on a daily basis. I was uncomfortable when I moved into the role of chief diversity officer and had to quickly come up to speed on current practices in that space. Sometimes, when we discuss topics that make us uncomfortable, we learn. Oftentimes, people are uncomfortable because they haven't had these types of inequality discussions with people of color. They're also afraid that the questions they may have will be offensive and are fearful of the repercussions of asking what they see as an innocent question.

But we need to allow for open and honest conversations so that we can better understand each other. Some questions should not be asked in a public forum, but if they're not meant to cause harm or mock a particular individual, they should be asked privately. Through exposure, we discover new insights, and those insights help us to create safe environments. Discomfort not only helps us focus on what matters, it also allows us to grow and create a work environment in which everyone can flourish. This is a win for the employees and for the company as well. It will have a positive impact on morale and job satisfaction, which will result in lower turnover rates.

As I contemplated taking on the additional responsibilities of serving as a chief diversity officer, my initial answer was "No," as I knew that in order to be effective in the role, I would need resources to make the necessary changes within the organization. I explained that if I were to serve as chief diversity officer, in addition to my full-time

HR responsibilities, I would need the talent acquisition team as a resource. The organization agreed.

The talent acquisition team would play an indispensable role in implementing the systemic changes needed to the hiring practices to ensure that the organization would meet its goal of diversifying the leadership. I felt that if I had the team reporting to me, they would be less resistant to the changes necessary. Typically, chief diversity officers have little more than administrative support and are tasked with lofty goals and limited resources. I did not want this to be me. (I cover the importance of resources for DEI Practitioners in Chapter 7.)

The Time I Got Fired

Although I take pride in my professional career, I was actually once fired for not going with the (discriminatory) flow. I can look back at it now and think of it as a learning experience, but at the time, I was infuriated.

I had received the highest category of performance rating. A couple of weeks after receiving my evaluation, I had a conversation with my leader, who said that the CEO wanted to know if we could terminate two African-American males who had filed Equal Employment Opportunity Council (EEOC) charges against the company. At that particular organization, we could terminate employees for any reason within a duration of time. I immediately called one of my team members and asked them to pull up those two employees' records. Both of them had been with the organization for several years and had stellar records, performance, and attendance. So, I told my leader no.

A few weeks later, my manager said they were changing my job. I was replaced with a White male who had a high school diploma. No college degree. Just a high school diploma. Although I hadn't reached the highest level of leadership at that point, I was still considered executive level. My consolation prize was keeping my pay and my title the same, but they basically gave me no job content and subsequently terminated me, stating to me in the conversation that they no longer had a spot for me on the team.

The purpose of sharing this story is to demonstrate how discrimination can occur. I could have done what I was asked to do and chucked it up to "just doing my job." But I wouldn't have been able to look at myself in the mirror, and that's what matters. If I have to convince myself that I didn't do anything wrong, then I probably did. I wouldn't have wanted someone to do that to me, so I reacted in the manner that I would have desired to be treated. Their termination was probably inevitable, true, but that didn't mean that I had to play a part in it. It was my responsibility to maintain our ethics, and that's what I did. The cost was ultimately my job, but as Ms. Lorraine said best, "To be the most effective leader you can be, you have to be okay with the worst possible outcome."

Let me add this one point. You have to continuously look at how your organization reproduces inequalities and upholds respectability politics, including awarding unearned inclusion. Ask questions like who isn't at the table, in what ways are our policies or culture forcing certain people to wear "masks," and what are the common denominators among those in positions of power? Are we fixing systems and actually healing the problem at the root, or are we only using a temporary fix? Longer-term solutions are more systemic in nature.

As an HR leader, I want cases that surface in the work environment presented to me in a fair and consistent manner. I want to know the name, title, how long they have been with the organization, demographic information, and any related facts. What does the policy state? What are our standard practices? Everyone has to be treated in a fair and consistent manner. This approach is one way to avoid double standards, biases, lawsuits, and bad press when it comes to hiring and firing. It takes a consistent review of all related data, a commitment to looking at the data from a demographic lens, and a willingness to address inequities.

#UseYourVoice

Working in HR gives me front-row seats to very personal stories that highlight how much jobs can restrict people from expressing their opinions, even when it feels as though they may have been directly kicked in the stomach. I have long since established a "rule" which allows any employee to schedule a meeting with me without having any advanced knowledge of the reason for the meeting request. I call these "no-subject" meetings. I typically find out when the requestor arrives, and I could face a range of emotions from tears to anger. I have heard stories about mistreatment in the workplace, and I always ask, "Did you say anything?" Many times, the response is no because of the fear of jeopardizing their job or retaliation from management.

I developed a workshop about microaggressions in the workplace. Microaggressions are commonplace daily verbal, behavioral, or environmental slights, whether intentional or unintentional, that communicate hostile, derogatory, or negative attitudes toward stigmatized or culturally marginalized groups."[14] If a non-Black person stands beside you quoting hip-hop lyrics, that could very well be a microaggression. Someone stretching their arm out beside yours to compare their summer tan to your natural brown skin is a microaggression.

In the workshop, I encouraged participants to prepare for a direct conversation with the perpetrator. The workshop concludes with each person being tasked with developing a hashtag articulating a way in which they plan to "use their voice." I have a stack of blank #UseYourVoice index cards, which I regularly distribute to people who visit my office who express a concern they should have addressed directly.

Stay True to Your Core

Show me someone who speaks up and stops the silence, and I'll show you someone who is true to their core. I often reflect that if I had allowed the terminations of those two Black men to take place, my career would have been stifled. I believe in spiritual consequence and karma: what goes around comes around. I strongly believe that I would've been punished or penalized in some way had I terminated employees for what I knew to be unjustified reasons. One of my workplace values consists of equal justice. I won't protect someone just because they're Black. My core values won't allow me to lie for anyone, regardless of race, gender, or economic background. On the other hand, I also won't stand by and watch the perpetration of unjust acts and stand in silence. I will speak up, and I encourage everyone to do so as well.

The company has its values, but what are yours? You'll naturally have values for yourself, your relationships, your work, etc. Many will overlap, and some will change with time and experience. It's important to have positive values that benefit everyone around us because they help make sure that we're heading toward a future in which it is more than just a word; it's a way of life. Whenever I hear the old saying, "Money can't buy happiness," I immediately think of values. Let's say your goal is to become a millionaire. If you abandon your values or never identify your values in your journey to reach that goal, then you'll likely make it there with a ton of regret, guilt, and bridges that may have been burned. There are many ways to achieve your goals. It's important not to leave a wake of destruction on your way to success.

Values motivate you to do the right thing for yourself and others. They serve as our moral compass. When you're on the job and are faced with a difficult decision, your values will help you make the decision that's in your best interest. One of my values, for instance, is assertiveness. I adopted this value while growing up in the inner city. I couldn't afford to allow myself to be bullied. My physical and social survivability depended on it.

So, when I say I'm bringing my full self to work, that assertiveness comes along with me. I don't beat around the bush; I approach challenges directly, always leading with professionalism. If I feel that a new policy negatively impacts one group more than others, I'll speak up and bring it to the attention of anyone who can do something about it. If I make a mistake, I'll admit it and do my best to correct it and not make the same mistake twice. I also don't mind saying no. This is very important. Oftentimes, we are in situations in which it is frowned upon to say no. You can be labeled a naysayer. That's a fine line to walk in corporate America because many executive leaders don't take too kindly to being told no.

You do, however, have to be prepared to support your position. Using your voice doesn't mean that management will always see things your way, but you will rest better knowing that you spoke up and tried to make a difference. And if this happens too often, you should consider seeking new employment in an environment that embraces diversity and is open to hearing differing opinions.

Respect is another value of mine. I do my best to always respect others as well as myself. This includes being extra mindful of what I say and how I say it. I practice active listening when people are talking to me. This means not interrupting them when they're speaking or preparing my response while they speak. It also means that they have my undivided attention.

As a representative in human resources, people come to me with all kinds of issues and concerns, many of which are private. They confide in me, and I respect their privacy. I also don't judge them for their questions or concerns.

I praise performance or behaviors that are applause-worthy and align with the company's core values. I empathize with those suffering, and I certainly never call anyone anything other than their name. Lastly, out of respect, I do my best to educate myself on different cultural practices to ensure that I don't mistakenly offend anyone with my words or actions.

Draw the Line

"Draw the line" is an old idiom that simply means creating boundaries or limiting what you will and won't do. It's putting your foot down and holding true to your beliefs. Like values, the lines that we draw serve as our compass. They also allow us to maintain our self-respect. One of the lines that I draw is regarding being cursed at or having someone talk to me in an offensive manner. I am conscious not to be condescending when speaking with people, and I demand that same respect when being addressed.

There was an incident in which a leader asked me about terminating an employee and whether HR would approve or deny the request. I explained that it was my first time hearing the employee's name and I would need to do some research before I could answer his question. He immediately said, in a public forum, that I needed to take my "ass" to a senior leader's office and tell him that I was going to be the "HR roadblock." Without a pause, I said to him, "No one speaks to me in that manner," and added a few words I'd rather not repeat. He immediately went on the defensive and said, "Calm down," as if I had started the exchange.

It was an unassuming Monday. Nothing was unusual about that day. I woke up, got dressed, drove to work, had a few meetings, and was doing what we all try to do on Monday . . . just get through it. We always complain about how the weekends are so short, but even if we had a four-day weekend, we'd find a way to complain. I guess that's just human nature in the corporate world.

Anyway, I happened to just wrap up a meeting and was sitting in my office preparing for my last meeting of the day when the same person who confronted me about the firing issue stormed into my office. He just stared at me until I looked up from my computer. When I looked up, I could see that he was visibly disturbed about something. Side note, barging into someone's office and staring at them with your arms crossed is never a good way to begin any discussion, but I digress. One of my key words is "silence." So, rather than picking up on his attitude and fueling his fire, I simply emotionlessly stared back at him. It was a tense few seconds (it felt like twenty, but it was probably closer to three), then he began to speak. He did not hold back.

He started yelling and was talking about how I made a decision in a vacuum, didn't take his input into consideration, and went over his head to resolve it. Now, I have to be honest. My first instinct was to stand up and tell him to get the h**l out of my office (not many people can state they have heard me even casually curse at the office, HR remember 😄), but I didn't, as that's what he would have been expecting.

This is another place for a quick sidebar. One thing that Blacks have to deal with is not being seen as the angry Black man or the angry Black woman. Many of my colleagues recount stories of being viewed as "angry" simply for expressing a counter-opinion. It's baffling, but that's the reality. So, rather than feed into this stereotype, I just sat there emotionless. I don't think I even blinked an eye until he finished. Then, when he finished his profanity-riddled rant, I remained silent for another few seconds before I spoke my first words, which were, "I understand your anger."

That reaction immediately caught him off guard. He came into my office expecting a fight, and young Ovell from Grand Rapids sure wanted to give him one, but I now have a new set of tools. I wasn't going to let him walk over me, but I was going to fight him with intellect. So, after my first sentence, I said, "Walking into my office with that attitude and behavior isn't going to get me to curl up in a corner and succumb to your request. Management by intimidation doesn't work in this office. So, let's start over, and I'll begin."

I explained to him the facts and the reasoning behind my decision, all in a calm and collected manner. That's another thing to remember. It's hard to fight people who aren't fighting back. I countered his anger with a calmness that neutralized the entire interaction. If you're the only one yelling, then at some point, you're going to stop yelling because it's awkward, particularly in a work environment.

He was visibly upset and probably geared himself up to have a bout with an angry Black man. What he got was a mature conversation with a calm and rational professional who knows how to listen and respond intellectually. See, what's important about this interaction is that I listened to him. It would have been easy for me to "hear" him yelling while preparing my argument and start yelling back when he finished, but I *listened* to him first, then I prepared my retort.

Now, had I been wrong, I would have admitted it and apologized in the same calm manner in which I offered my true response, and the result, at the end of the day, would have been the same. He understood my point and simply asked to be looped in should this type of situation happen again. I agreed, shook his hand, and he left. He probably left with the same "result" he expected to leave with when he entered my office, but the journey to that result was far off of his intended route.

We eventually found common ground and were able to have more adult conversations, and he never harshly interacted with me like that ever again. I remember thinking that I should have addressed his behavior early on, and maybe a lot of this could have been avoided, but I didn't have all of the tools to do so. People will push you until you push back. Use your voice and let them know early on that you have boundaries that should not be crossed. That will make your interactions more productive and save everyone time and energy that could be better used to solving problems.

In summary, define your parameters, then decide the actions you will take when they are crossed. Which lines won't you allow someone to cross? If someone hits you, are you going to hit them back? If someone makes an inaccurate statement, are you correcting them before they get to the next word? One thing I will always do is protect my team. If someone says something unfair about my team, I'm going to correct them. Regardless of the forum, I want my team to know that I support them, and even if they make a mistake, I will address it with constructive feedback, always treating people with dignity and respect.

CHAPTER 7

SYSTEMS VS. CHARITY
(EMPLOYERS)

I Need a Fork!

I magine sitting at a restaurant waiting for the meal you ordered and realizing after it arrives that you have no utensils, including the "coveted" fork. You could probably make some progress without the fork, but depending on the meal, you might begin to face many challenges. I liken this scenario to what happens when companies do not commit the necessary resources to support DEI efforts. Many diverse team members are asked to support company efforts and find themselves handcuffed without the necessary resources. Even individuals who have been named chief diversity officers have found themselves with little more than an administrative assistant. The work is already daunting, and companies should be mindful of equipping their leaders of diversity with the necessary tools to be impactful.

In addition, the models we see across the corporate landscape include asking employees to lead diversity councils and inclusion resource groups, adding significant additional responsibilities, often with no supplemental compensation. It runs the risk of sending a message of not valuing the work.

As the chief diversity officer for the organization that agreed to resource me with the talent acquisition team, I was responsible for both the recruitment and diversity teams; both were led by directors who reported to me. As a collective group, because we were adequately staffed, we were able to develop and cultivate community partnerships and work in tandem to implement action plans to address affirmative action reviews. We worked to identify and apply systemic changes in hiring, which led to an increase in our leadership diversity in one year by 29 percent.

As a government contractor, the organization was required to put forth good faith efforts to make sure the organization reflected the diverse populations of our community. (Examples of good faith efforts could include recruitment from HBCUs, development of a leadership program for minorities and women to advance them into higher level positions, etc.) A neutral party audits these contracting companies' workforce demographics by position level and determines if the company needs to establish goals to be more reflective of the diversity that is present in their communities. If that is the case, a typical practice is to develop a recruitment or hiring strategy to address the gap, which is exactly what my team did.

Some of our successful systemic changes included requiring diverse candidate slates, panel-based interviews, hiring leaders formally trained in interviewing techniques, including bias, and utilizing skill-based interview guides. Having a structure for interviewing and requiring panels and guides helps reduce the bias that occurs. It's imperative to review each step in the hiring process (sourcing, screening, selection, onboarding) and fix all of the barriers and systems as key contributors to positive outcomes.

As I mentioned earlier, I refused to be a chief diversity officer who lacked resources. That would've been tokenism at its finest, and I'm not interested in holding a position that has no power to influence change. For me to agree to assume the additional responsibilities, I needed to be able to actually make a difference. Because I was equipped with a "fork" (the partnering teams), we were able to identify and implement systemic change that didn't just affect one or two individuals but the existing staff, those yet to be hired, and the organization as a whole.

Politics

There is a political element to corporate America that almost resembles a campaign. When you really think about it, companies will lay out the red carpet during the recruiting process. People say a lot of things and make a lot of promises when lobbying for that vote, but like my grandmother used to say, "Teeth and tongue will say anything." Similarly, companies put their best foot forward to secure the best, most qualified candidates. They talk about promotional opportunities from within, but what is concealed is how diversity thins out at the higher leadership levels of the corporate ladder. They present you with a great compensation and benefits package and tell you all about their core values and thriving corporate culture. However, what they might fail to disclose is the actual lack of diversity despite the appearance of such on the company website and marketing materials.

Just like some politicians, some companies tell you whatever you want to hear or whatever sounds good, particularly when under pressure or duress, still, you must pay close attention to the actions behind the words. Consequently, one of the problems in corporate settings is that words don't always match behaviors. It is important for the mission statement and the core values to match how you are operating as a corporation or business entity.

Many of us have taken a Diversity, Equity, and Inclusion (DEI) training at some point in our careers. Unfortunately, companies invest tens of thousands of dollars on these trainings, presentations, and workshops with very little change in the actual inner workings, such as policy changes, hiring processes, and promotional opportunities.

DEI goes beyond a simple training video or workshop. It should be an ongoing effort that really involves the willingness of an entire company or corporation, not just the underrepresented. It takes dedication and commitment to implement systems that lead to better outcomes for all.

The "Data Challenge"

Data should be used as the catalyst for addressing diversity issues in the workplace. We're an evidence-based society, and data is the key to making sound systemic recommendations. The answers to what the company is doing wrong are found in employee-related metrics. Where's recruitment taking place, who's being interviewed, who's being hired and who isn't, who's being written up and for what, who's being promoted and who's not, who's being terminated, etc.? You need more people who understand the sources of data and can make sure that those sources can be interpreted. Specifically, as it relates to those who are willing to stop the silence, when they know what the numbers mean, the data can be used to support recommendations.

Often, these change agents will run into the "data challenge." That is, the roadblocks or barriers to progress created by individuals who challenge the source of data and even the data itself. They use the "data challenge" as a means of covering up the fact that they may not be supportive of diversity efforts. They could state, "I don't understand the numbers, or are you sure the numbers are correct?" Those are the individuals to pay attention to in the conversations. These seemingly innocent challenges can add unnecessary time in implementing proactive measures to address inequities.

I am a proponent of making systemic recommendations to address root causes leading to disparities in outcomes we see in data. My focus in the work is on policies, procedures, and practices. I refer to those as the "three Ps." Policies need to be reviewed to ensure they are not leading to inequities. Many policies have continued to exist without regular review and are not aligned to reflect current workplace practices. Procedures are just as important as written policies. For example, if an organization has a procedure in place that does not allow for diverse perspectives to be considered, it could lead to an offensive ad, which could be irreparably damaging to a company's reputation. I always highlight the point that if the policies and procedures that you have formalized are not being enforced or practiced, it could lead to unfavorable outcomes.

DEI work typically garners more support for addressing "charitable" components, such as addressing a short-term need. As the conversations shift to the systems, less support occurs. Organizations have to be willing to determine root causes and fix systems. Staunch diversity advocates want immediate change, but systemic changes take longer to see results. It all begins with acknowledging that there is an issue that needs to be addressed. This begins at the top of the organization, and all leaders have to be on the same page and be willing to move forward in lockstep to make changes. Until that happens, no progress can be made.

Once the problems have been identified, you have to group them into two categories: short-term and long-term. Short-term changes are often called low-hanging fruit. These are the ones in which immediate action can be taken. For example, you can look at your organization and see if there are BIPOC employees who deserve to be promoted and put on a fast track to executive leadership roles. Long-term initiatives could include requiring that both internal and external recruiters provide a diverse candidate pool. You can also join minority organizations and attend job fairs at the various HBCUs or Black professional organizations such as the National Black MBA Association in order to find candidates from different sources. These take more time and effort, but if you are willing to take the appropriate steps, the benefits far out-weigh the costs.

In summary, systemic changes take longer for the re-sults to be realized. It is not okay to avoid conversations about root causes. Everyone must be committed to the long-term investment of fixing the "three Ps"—policies, procedures, and practices.

KEEP MOVING!

How Will You Be Remembered?

Don't just breeze by that question. I want you to actually take a second to pause and reflect. No one wants to be the person lying in a box in the front of the church listening to accolades or "remarks" and finding themselves in stark disagreement with the words expressed.

Regardless of your role in the company, you have a moral responsibility to stop the silence, lest, as author and anthropologist Zora Neale Hurston said best, "They'll kill you and say you enjoyed it." Use your voice. That's the core message of this book. Speak up, blow the whistle, throw the flag, tell your truth. Your voice is your power. And stay true to your core. What do you believe, and what's most important to you? Stand up for that. That's how you create a legacy with which you can truly rest in peace.

Many of us are placed in various situations, and we adapt based upon the environment. I had never really considered myself to be a people pleaser, but in my effort to be an effective leader and valuable team player, my ability to adapt stretched far beyond my limits. My job duties required global responsibilities, which meant that I had to be accessible around the clock. Since I was so dedicated to my work, I sacrificed my health and well-being, which resulted in a broken ankle, a bleeding ulcer, and overall exhaustion. There was a point in my career when I had to ask myself: How will I be remembered?

I was deeply bothered by the nurses' and doctors' comments when I was hospitalized for the ulcers. Their comments made me reflect on how I would be remembered when my time does come. Most of the answers would have referenced a successful career, and I would have cringed with every utterance of those words. I decided that, once I healed, I would become the author of the answer to that question.

The experience contributed to me taking ownership of what others would say by making substantial life changes. As I mentioned, growing up in Grand Rapids and excelling academically but needing a lot of financial assistance to pursue my higher education, many non-profit organizations provided me with scholarships. I decided to repay all of the non-profit scholarship money that had been provided to me, mostly from organizations from the city of Grand Rapids. Most were shocked as I contacted them to tell them that I was paying it forward. One organization even asked me to serve as their keynote speaker. I used my first marathon to raise money for one of the organizations and subsequently paid back the rest through my personal savings account. For the one organization which was no longer in existence, I developed a "Plan B" approach.

In addition to the "payback," I wanted to invest in others as others had invested in me, which led me to establish the Barbee Book Club. I regularly select students who have a compelling story to tell me and agree to cover four years of books and supplies while the students are in college. I tell them that I expect them to remember the gesture and to be willing to invest in someone else in the future. Many of my closest friends were unaware that I was doing this when I first started the book club. I wasn't doing it for the recognition. I was doing it because, to me, it was the right thing to do. Period. And as Dr. Martin Luther King, Jr. said best, "The time is always right to do what is right."

In the beginning of this book, I referenced the park across the street from the house where I was raised. It was initially called Franklin Park, and after the death of Dr. Martin Luther King Jr., the name was changed to MLK to honor his legacy. As a child, I would write about him regularly, so it was only fitting that I recognize him as I write about my leadership journey. I was asked to speak about one of his quotes, "If you can't fly, then run. If you can't run, then walk. If you can't walk, then crawl, but whatever you do, you have to keep moving," at the community-wide MLK Day celebration in 2020.

I would like to end by sharing my words.[15]

"If you can't fly, then run. If you can't run, then walk. If you can't walk, then crawl, but whatever you do, you have to keep moving."

For me, it all starts with a vision. My grandmother used to say, "You have to crawl before you can walk." Dr. King's quote continues with an interesting sequence of reduced speed—from flying to running to walking to crawling. However, the one word the quote does not mention is STOP. Those words from Dr. King were meant to suggest we should keep moving forward until we reach our goal or shared vision to be more inclusive and equitable for all members. If this is truly a "shared" vision, then we must all work together to ensure that work is underway to achieve the goal. This means that all of us need to use our voices to push for change.

I have always appreciated the reflection that comes with the start of a new year. 2020 means we should all have stellar "vision" or a stellar vision as we look to make our community more inclusive. I don't want to be controversial, but some of our community headlines ending the previous decade were not favorable and would suggest that we have lots of work still ahead.

Silence is not an option! The conversations can be uncomfortable and emotionally charged as we speak about diversity, equity, and inclusion. Racism, discrimination, harassment, and bullying are all words that are not intended to be "nice" by definition. Each of these words comes with an element of hate and bias.

Dr. King wasn't asking us to do anything that was beyond our capabilities. His words are metaphors for determination and perseverance. Don't quit. Move forward. Never stop pursuing your dream, our collective dream. That's not a difficult ask, and I think that when you focus on the true essence of his words, you understand what he is trying to accomplish, which is simply to motivate us, as a community, to keep our eyes on the prize and to continue to move our people forward.

We are fortunate to live in an age in which we have choices. Others who went before us had no choice as they endured lashes on their backs for trying to learn to read, the bites of vicious dogs as they attempted to vote, having the skin ripped and torn from their bodies by powerful fire hoses as they marched for freedom; the same freedom that you and I and our children enjoy today. Reading, Voting, Freedom!

What sacrifices are you willing to make? Others who came before us sacrificed a lot. You heard some harsh examples. Dr. King, he sacrificed his life. Did you complain about the snow as you gazed through the window from your heated home this weekend? You have that option because others sacrificed their lives to make sure that their children and grandchildren and generations to come wouldn't have to live in the horrific conditions to which they were subjected. It is time to continue pushing for change!

My challenge to you is to do all that you can to make this community better. We ALL can do something. We may not be able to "fly," but to make a difference, all you have to do is move forward and not stop.

NEVER . . . STOP . . . MOVING . . . FORWARD! Crawl, walk, run, and then fly! The vision is possible!

Thank you.

FINAL THOUGHTS

Many people would ask me, "How did I do it?" The book for me highlights some of the key milestones that helped me grow my career and develop as a leader. I do not take for granted how very fortunate I have been. I am indeed an advocate on behalf of those who do not sit at the same tables at which I have been fortunate enough to have a seat. I embrace the assignment of advocating on behalf of those who need advocacy.

We can build better communities and can change lives! Raise your hand! Use your voice!

Stop the silence!

ENDNOTES

1. Holloway, Jenae. "White People: Your Comfort Is Not Our Problem." Vogue. Vogue, June 11, 2020. https://www.vogue.com/article/white-people-your-comfort-is-not-my-problem-black-lives-matter.

2. Rosenthal, Caitlin. "From Plantation to Corporation." Social Science Matrix. Berkeley University of California, October 2, 2014. https://matrix.berkeley.edu/research-article/plantation-corporation/.

3. Aragão, Carolina. "Gender Pay Gap in U.S. Hasn't Changed Much in Two Decades." Pew Research Center. Pew Research Center, March 1, 2023. https://www.pewresearch.org/fact-tank/2021/05/25/gender-pay-gap-facts/.

4. Dewar, Jen. "8 Wage Gap Statistics to Know in 2022." Compaas. Compaas, February 21, 2023. https://www.compa.as/blog/wage-gap-statistics.

5. Smith, Ember, and Richard V. Reeves. "SAT Math Scores Mirror and Maintain Racial Inequity." Brookings. Brookings, March 9, 2022. https://www.brookings.edu/blog/up-front/

2020/12/01/sat-math-scores-mirror-and-maintain-racial-inequity/.

6. McCluney, Courtney L., Kathrina Robotham, Serenity Lee, Richard Smith, and Myles Durkee. "The Costs of Code-Switching." Harvard Business Review, January 28, 2021. https://hbr.org/2019/11/the-costs-of-codeswitching.

7. McCall, Nathan. *Makes Me Wanna Holler: A Young Black Man in America*. New York, NY: Random House, 2016.

8. Dunbar, Paul Laurence. "We Wear the Mask by Paul Laurence Dunbar - Poems | Academy of American Poets." Poets.org. Academy of American Poets. Accessed September 20, 2022. https://poets.org/poem/we-wear-mask.

9. DuBois, W. E. Burghardt. "The Health and Physique of the Negro American. 1906." American journal of public health. U.S. National Library of Medicine, February 2003. https://www.ncbi.nlm.nih.gov/pmc/articles/PMC1449799/.

10. Caruso, PhD, RN, Claire, and Roger R. Rosa, PhD R Rosa, PhD. "Sleep and Work." Centers for Disease Control and Prevention. Centers for Disease Control and Prevention, March 8, 2012. https://blogs.cdc.gov/niosh-science-blog/2012/03/08/sleep-and-work/.

11. Barajas, Clara B., Shawn C. Jones, Adam J. Milam, Roland J. Thorpe, Darrell J. Gaskin, Thomas A. LaVeist, and C. Debra Furr-Holden. "Coping, Discrimination, and Physical Health Conditions among Predominantly Poor, Urban African Americans: Implications for Community-Level Health Services."

Journal of Community Health 44, no. 5 (October 26, 2019): 954–62. https://doi.org/10.1007/s10900-019-00650-9.

12. Lee, Brandy X. "Structural Violence - Violence - Wiley Online Library." Wiley Online Library. Wiley, March 1, 2019. https://onlinelibrary.wiley.com/doi/10.1002/9781119240716.ch7.

13. Parker, Kim, and Juliana Menasce Horowitz. "Majority of Workers Who Quit a Job in 2021 Cite Low Pay, No Opportunities for Advancement, Feeling Disrespected." Pew Research Center. Pew Research Center, March 10, 2022. https://www.pewresearch.org/fact-tank/2022/03/09/majority-of-workers-who-quit-a-job-in-2021-cite-low-pay-no-opportunities-for-advancement-feeling-disrespected/.

14. Sue, Derald Wing. "The Manifestation of Racial, Gender, and Sexual-Orientation Microaggression." Chapter. In *Microaggressions in Everyday Life*, xvi. Hoboken, NJ: Wiley, 2010.

15. Barbee Jr., Ovell. "Keep Moving" (lecture, DeVos Place, Grand Rapids, MI, January 20, 2020.

ABOUT THE AUTHOR

Ovell R. Barbee, Jr. is compassionately assertive in righting wrongs and using his voice to challenge the status quo on behalf of others. An HR executive and chief diversity officer at Fortune 500 companies and renowned health systems, he's been named a Top-100 Chief Diversity Officer by the National Diversity Council, and a Top 50 Under 50 Executive by the National Black MBA Association, among other honors.

Growing up in inner-city Grand Rapids, Michigan, Barbee excelled academically, earning scholarships that helped him achieve a bachelor's in communications and a master's in social work from University of Michigan, Ann Arbor, and a master's in labor relations and human resources from Michigan State University.

Barbee gave back to the community by repaying all the scholarship money he received. He also established the "Barbee Book Club," which pays for books and supplies for four years of college for a local Grand Rapids student.

CREATING DISTINCTIVE BOOKS
WITH INTENTIONAL RESULTS

We're a collaborative group of creative masterminds
with a mission to produce high-quality books to position
you for monumental success in the marketplace.

Our professional team of writers, editors, designers,
and marketing strategists work closely together to ensure
that every detail of your book is a clear representation
of the message in your writing.

Want to know more?
Write to us at info@publishyourgift.com
or call (888) 949-6228

Discover great books, exclusive offers, and more at
www.PublishYourGift.com

Connect with us on social media

@publishyourgift

Printed in the USA
CPSIA information can be obtained
at www.ICGtesting.com
JSHW012014141123
52031JS00004B/15

9 781644 846247